Inefficient Market Theory

An Investment Framework Based on the Foolishness of the Crowd

By: Jeffrey C Hood

Founder and Managing Member

Austin Value Capital, LLC

ISBN: 0692273948

ISBN-13: 978-0692273944

Library of Congress Control Number: 2014914852

CreateSpace Independent Publishing Platform

North Charleston, South Carolina

Dedication

This book is dedicated to my wife Brenda and my wonderful children Hannah, Carsten, and Amelia, whose love and support made this possible.

THANK YOU

I would particularly like to thank my partner at Austin Value Capital, Joel Stevens, for his friendship, intelligent discussions and insightful commentary and revisions. I would also like to thank my colleague Mark Williams for our many discussions on investment and psychology.

ACKNOWLEDGEMENT

Most of this book was written while perched on the coast of Washington state's Olympic Peninsula, with the waves crashing about me. There is no better place for thought or introspection.

TABLE OF CONTENTS

TERMINOLOGY

In *Security Analysis*, Benjamin Graham devoted an entire chapter to the issue of clearly defining the term "Investing." Graham's definitions of an investment are set out below:

> An investment operation is one, which upon thorough analysis, promises safety of principal and a satisfactory return. Operations not meeting these requirements are speculative.[1]

> An investment operation is one that can be justified on *both* qualitative and quantitative grounds.[2]

For the best understanding of these definitions, the reader is highly encouraged to read Chapter 4 of *Security Analysis*, Sixth Edition. However, a few salient points should be noted here. First is the use of the term "upon thorough analysis." Graham defined "thorough analysis" as "the study of the facts in light of established standards of safety and value."[3] Graham believed in the idea of appraising the value of a business on both qualitative and quantitative grounds, and only purchasing securities that were priced well below that assessed value. Only purchases made on such terms were capable of promising "safety of principal and a satisfactory return."

In this book the term "market participant" is generally used to refer to people who buy and sell stocks in the stock market, both individual and professional alike. For professionals who manage stock portfolios on behalf of others, the term "professional money manager" is also often used. Conventional investment literature and the financial media, on the other hand, tend to refer to everyone as "investors." We believe that: 1) the term "investor" should be reserved for those who practice the art of "investing"; and 2) many who are called, or believe themselves to be, investors are actually speculators. This distinction is extremely important – nothing could be more misleading than the belief that all purchases of securities are investments. For both individuals and professionals alike, not knowing the difference between investment and speculation, or the belief that one is investing when he is in fact speculating, is extremely harmful. By reserving use of the term "investor" only when actual investment operations are discussed, this book hopes to do its part in attempting to dispel the myth that all security purchases are investments, and all market participants are investors.

INTRODUCTION

The world of stock market investing has two main camps: active management (or active investing) and passive management (or passive investing). Active management involves the active selection of individual stocks, or groups of stocks, with the expectation that these stock selections will outperform the overall market, or will outperform certain benchmark indexes such as the S&P 500. Active management inherently presumes that the stock market is not completely efficient and hence that various individual stocks are at least occasionally mispriced in the market. Active management also presumes that with the application of sufficient knowledge, skill and experience one can reliably identify these mispriced securities and take advantage of these market inefficiencies to earn superior returns relative to the market / indexes.

Passive management, on the other hand, generally refers to the purchase of various types of index funds (including both index mutual funds and Exchange Traded Funds, most of which are indexed). An index fund is a fund with a fixed portfolio of stocks that is constructed to match or track a market index. A passive investment strategy using index funds can be analogized to a plane being flown on autopilot, whereas in an active investment strategy a pilot is at the controls. A primary benefit of passive investment strategies using index funds is lower frictional costs, i.e., lower operating expenses (since the investor is not paying someone to actively select stocks) and lower taxation costs, primarily due to the lower portfolio turnover. Passive management is inherently based on the premise that markets are efficient, or at least sufficiently efficient such that the marginal benefit of actively selecting stocks (the marginal profit made on an active strategy over a passive one) does not exceed the marginal costs of active management. More formally, passive management is based on the Efficient Market Theory (EMT), which essentially says that information relating to businesses is widely disseminated and immediately incorporated by rational market participants into stock prices, thus producing stock prices that are always the "correct" prices. Hence, according to EMT, it is impossible to reliably and consistently "beat the market" through active stock selection.

The decision as to whether an investor should choose an active or passive management style for his stock portfolio essentially comes down to the following questions:

1) Is it theoretically possible to actively manage a stock portfolio and consistently and reliably obtain superior returns over a passive strategy? In other words, a) is the stock market inefficient? and b) do these inefficiencies correct themselves in a sufficiently reliable manner to profit from them?

2) If so, does the respective individual investor have sufficient knowledge, skill, experience, and by far most importantly of all, the right temperament, to identify and act on these mispriced securities and attain these superior returns; or does he think he can properly select a professional manager who can do this for him?

The first portion of this book addresses the first question above, which we answer in the affirmative. First, we introduce the concept of the "wisdom of the crowd", which is the intellectual basis underlying Efficient Market Theory. We then explore whether crowd wisdom applies to a financial marketplace, such as the stock market. In doing so, we identify a number of criteria that must be satisfied in order for the wisdom of the crowd to apply. We then analyze these criteria in the context of a financial marketplace and find that a number of these criteria are simply not met.

Benjamin Graham addressed the first question above in his landmark classic "Security Analysis", where he stated:

> This field of analytical work [discovery of undervalued and overvalued securities] may be said to rest upon

a twofold assumption: first, that the market price is frequently out of line with the true value; and, second, that there is an inherent tendency for those disparities to correct themselves. As to the truth of the former statement, there can be very little doubt – even though Wall Street often speaks glibly of the 'infallible judgment of the market' and asserts that 'a stock is worth what you can sell it for – neither more nor less.'[4]

Graham thus clearly thought that the market was inefficient and did not always produce correct prices. What we will see is that the reason that financial markets remain decidedly inefficient is because of one thing that has not changed and likely never will – human nature.

With respect to Graham's second assumption – that incorrect stock prices inherently tend to correct themselves over time – he commented that this "is equally true in theory, but its working out in practice is often most unsatisfactory." Here Graham noted that in his day undervaluation of stocks could "persist for an inconveniently long time" and thus there was always the danger that "new determining factors may supervene before the market price adjusts itself to the value [determined by the analyst]." Today we benefit from the fact that the markets are perhaps more responsive in reacting to inconsistencies between price and value than in Graham's day. This is largely due to the much greater amount of information available to market participants, the improved means of distributing this information (e.g., the Internet), and the superior tools available to modern investors (e.g., the computer, spreadsheets and various stock screening tools).

In our analysis, we address both of Graham's assumptions in the first question posed above. Our analysis of crowd wisdom criteria will demonstrate exactly why the wisdom of the crowd does not operate in a financial marketplace to uniformly produce correct prices. Performing the above exercise will help us understand why and where financial markets are inefficient. Even further, our attempts to identify exactly how this inefficiency, what we call the "Foolishness of the Crowd", manifests itself in stock prices will aid in understanding the nature of the second assumption Graham presented above – why incorrect stock prices tend to return to correct values over the long term.

Our discussion of the first question posed above – whether successful active management is possible – will also help us understand how best to take advantage of these inefficiencies, thus providing some assistance to the second question posed above – how to identify and take advantage of mispriced securities and become a successful investor. One of the fundamental ideas in this book is that an understanding of the various criteria that are not met in attempting to apply the wisdom of the crowd to a financial marketplace produces remarkable insights as to: 1) the particular reasons why the stock market is not efficient; and 2) where to look in the market for these mispricings. Armed with these insights, the remainder of the book then explores how an investor can best take advantage of these inefficiencies to produce superior returns in the market.

In particular, the second part of the book introduces an investment framework for stock selection based on three components. The first component is the development of a "variant perception" – a contrarian view of the value of a business that differs from the market's view. The variant perception is established by a fundamental qualitative and quantitative assessment of the value of the business to determine if its valuation is sufficiently different from the market price to warrant investment. The second component is a new concept we introduce referred to as the "inefficient rationale." The inefficient rationale is the investor's reasoned explanation, based on his newfound understanding of the criteria needed for crowd wisdom to manifest, as to exactly *why* the market is not producing the correct price in a particular situation. As we will see, the inefficient rationale will generally be based on principles of psychology and crowd behavior, as well as various systemic forces present in the market that give rise to inefficiencies. We believe that the development of an inefficient rationale is a critical component to any investment framework, as it provides a key understanding of why the crowd (the market) is not producing a wise result. The third component of our investment framework is an intelligent cloning strategy that analyzes and selectively copies the investments of other great value investors. This cloning strategy draws its strength from the powerful force of crowd wisdom, but in this case a smaller, wiser crowd that is selected specifically both for 1) its skill and ability to generate correct variant perceptions; and 2) its immunity to irrationality. In effect, this cloning strategy selects a smaller, more intelligent crowd that is much less susceptible to the psychological inefficiencies of the larger market.

We provide some examples of this investment framework in operation, and we explore aspects of this framework in the context of macroeconomic crises and stock market bubbles. Another fundamental idea we explore is, given recent advances in behavioral finance and our understanding of why crowd wisdom does not manifest in a financial marketplace, whether the irrationality of the crowd is sufficiently predictable in its own right to act as the sole basis for identification and selection of mispriced securities.

PART I. THE CROWD IN A FINANCIAL MARKETPLACE

1. THE WISDOM OF THE CROWD

The "wisdom of the crowd" is the idea that an averaged collection of a large number of independent, informed decisions or opinions of a diverse group of rational individuals is likely to be much better than the decision of any single individual, or even that of any expert. The notion is that the crowd comprises a large number of diverse individuals, each with his own viewpoint, background, education, experience set, etc. Each person provides his particular slant or interpretation to the information at hand, producing a unique estimate or decision. If the crowd is sufficiently large, it can be presumed that substantially equal numbers of people are providing estimates at corresponding ranges both above and below the correct number, and thus the average of these estimates should approximate the correct answer.

Consider a simple example involving a large jar containing an unknown number of jelly beans. If any one person were to guess the number of jelly beans in the jar, the guess would likely be quite poor. If a hundred people were to each make an independent guess of how many jelly beans were in the jar, and these guesses were collectively averaged, the result would most likely be better than any individual's guess. If ten thousand people were to each make an independent guess of how many jelly beans were in the jar, the average of these guesses would be much better still, and would likely be very close to being correct.

A real world example of the wisdom of the crowd at work is the story of the contest observed by Francis Galton in 1906. Galton was visiting a livestock fair where a contest was being held involving an ox that was on display. The villagers were invited to guess the animal's weight after it was slaughtered and dressed, and those with the most accurate guesses received prizes. Nearly 800 villagers participated, many of whom held related experience, either from their work with livestock or past participation in similar contests. After the contest was over and the results tabulated, Galton observed to his surprise that "the middlemost estimate expresses the *vox populi* [the voice of the people], every other estimate being condemned as too low or too high by a majority of the voters."[5] Galton calculated the median of the estimates and discovered that the median (1,207 pounds) was within 0.8% of the measured weight (1,198 pounds). He also later discovered[6] that the mean of the guesses (1,197 pounds) was even more accurate.[7]

A more recent example of crowd wisdom comes from the field of seismic analysis. Here an oil exploration company published its seismic data and offered a large prize to the company that produced the best drilling location estimate based on analysis of this data. A number of seismic companies accepted the challenge and provided their results to the exploration company. However, instead of merely selecting what it thought was the best individual drilling location estimate, the exploration company averaged the results from all of the seismic companies and chose to drill in the resulting location. The exploration company later determined that this location, the average of all of the provided location estimates, was the optimal drilling location – better than any of the individual drilling location estimates. The company awarded the prize to the seismic company whose drilling estimate was closest to this averaged location.[8]

The rising popularity of "crowdsourcing" perhaps most clearly displays the benefits of crowd wisdom. Crowdsourcing is the act of outsourcing a task to the crowd, i.e., "taking a job traditionally performed by a designated agent (usually an employee) and outsourcing it to an undefined, generally large group of people in the form of an open call." One type of crowdsourcing relies on the wisdom of the crowd. This form of crowdsourcing collects information from a large group of people and aggregates this information to obtain a more accurate answer to a question. This "wisdom of the crowd" crowdsourcing is based on the idea that the combined knowledge of a large group of people is better than that of any single individual. This idea of collective intelligence is particularly effective when conducted on the Internet because a large group of people from diverse backgrounds can contribute in real-time within the same forum.

What type of result can we expect from the "wisdom of the crowd"? In an ideal scenario, crowd wisdom will always produce "correct" answers, or at least answers that are within a very narrow range of the correct answers. However, depending on the size, make-up, and character of the crowd this expectation may not be justified. More reasonably, crowd wisdom may not always produce correct answers, and in fact may seldom produce the correct answer, but it will generally produce a much better answer than any single individual could reliably and consistently provide.

To summarize the "wisdom of the crowd", if a large number of independent (or uncorrelated) opinions or estimates are obtained from a large, diverse group of rational people, and these estimates are averaged, the result will be a much better answer than any single person's opinion, and will likely be very close to being correct.

Certain criteria are required for the wisdom of the crowd to be present, i.e., for the crowd to produce a reliably correct result. In the book titled "Wisdom of the Crowds: Why the Many are Smarter Than the Few and How Collective Wisdom Shapes Business, Economies, Societies and Nations", James Surowiecki explores the wisdom of crowds and acknowledges that not all crowds (groups) produce wisdom. Surowiecki sets forth four characteristics necessary for a crowd to be deemed wise, and describes them as follows:

1. Diversity of opinion – each person should have private information even if it is just an eccentric interpretation of the known facts.

2. Independence – people's opinions are not determined by the opinions of those around them.

3. Decentralization – People are able to specialize and draw on local knowledge.

4. Aggregation – Some mechanism exists for turning private judgments into a collective decision.

In addition to these four criteria, Surowiecki implicitly introduces a fifth requirement, noting in his book that the crowd must also possess some minimal amount of knowledge or information as to what they are opining on. Surowiecki explains:

> At heart, the answer rests on a mathematical truism. If you ask a large enough group of diverse, independent people to make a prediction or estimate a probability, and then average those estimates, the errors each of them makes in coming up with an answer will cancel themselves out. Each person's guess, you might say, has two components: information and error. Subtract the error, and you're left with the information.

> Now, even with the errors canceled out, it's possible that a group's judgment will be bad. For the group to be smart, there has to be at least some information in the 'information' part of the 'information minus error' equation.

Perhaps Surowiecki did not include this fifth "information" requirement because there is a tendency to believe that crowd members inherently have sufficient knowledge or information to provide informed judgments upon most any issue. After all, the requirement that members of the crowd have "at least some information" does not seem particularly onerous. However, as the difficulty of a question increases, an increasing number of the members of the crowd may not have the requisite information, or the proper analytical framework, to produce informed opinions. Thus it seems that we should explicitly add "information" to our requirements for the applicability of crowd wisdom.

Let's briefly analyze each of the above criteria. Diversity of opinion is virtually inherent in most environments. Every person comes to the table with at least a slightly different background, education and set of experiences. Accordingly, each person will interpret the facts at hand based on his unique perspective. Independence is clearly an important criterion, as otherwise people would be influenced by other's opinions, and a herd mentality would develop (more on this later). The third criterion of decentralization relates to the problem of hierarchical organizations and bureaucracies wherein upper levels in the hierarchy are able to squelch the wisdom of those at the bottom of the hierarchy. The author provides as an example the Columbia shuttle disaster, which he blames on a hierarchical management bureaucracy at NASA that ignored the opinions of low-level engineers. The fourth criterion of aggregation is not really a requirement of the people forming the crowd, but rather relates to the notion that in the overall framework or structure in which the crowd operates there must be some mechanism for turning a number of private judgments into a collective decision or estimate. The implicit requirement of information can also be presumed to be inherent in many environments where a crowd operates. However, it certainly cannot be taken for granted. Upon reflection it is fairly easy to imagine scenarios where a crowd is providing a collective judgment where a large number of the members of the crowd lack adequate information or knowledge to provide informed judgements. Political elections and juries in complex cases come to mind here.

Given that the focus of this book is on the operation of crowds in financial markets, I propose a slightly enhanced set of criteria that I believe are critical for a crowd to provide collective wisdom in such an environment. Below I have proposed some additional criteria not mentioned by Surowiecki, likely because he presumed they were inherent in most any crowd. However, in a financial marketplace nothing can be assumed or taken for granted. The criteria set out below are very likely not exhaustive, i.e., there may be and likely are other factors which would be necessary. However, each of these criteria is absolutely required for crowd wisdom to manifest. The criteria below would likely have broad applicability in various decision-making scenarios, but would certainly be important, indeed critical, for collective wisdom to surface in a financial marketplace.

1. Incentives: the proper incentives are in place for people to provide the correct answer.

2. Independence: the decisions are independent – each person is not aware of or affected by the decisions of others.

3. Diversity of Opinion: the people have sufficiently different backgrounds, education, experience, and/or knowledge such that a diversity of opinion is provided.

4. Decentralization: the people are able to make their decisions without bureaucratic or systemic constraints.

5. Knowledge: the people generally have at least a modicum of knowledge or experience, and utilize an appropriate analytical framework, that allows them to provide some type of informed estimate or opinion.

6. Rationality: the people making the decisions think in a rational manner in formulating their opinions.

Let's analyze the above requirements for the wisdom of the crowd to take effect in an environment such as a financial marketplace.

First, the people involved must have the proper incentives to provide correct answers. Incentives are a powerful force in human conduct – there is no more fundamental idea in economics and human behavior than the notion that people respond to, and adjust their conduct based on, incentives. When the objective is to guess the number of jelly beans in a jar, and a prize is being offered for the best answer, the incentive is clearly to provide the correct answer. Similarly, in many scenarios that one can imagine, the incentive would be for people to provide, to the best of their ability, correct estimates. However, markets are quite complex, and the incentives for many of the participants are often less than clear. In financial markets the primary incentive seemingly is to make money, which is not necessarily the same as correctly estimating stock prices. In particular, for professional money managers operating in a financial market the true incentives may be selfish ones, such as maximizing personal income, job security, career advancement, etc., which may not completely align with the goal of moving stock prices to their correct values. Incentives are an important consideration in virtually any human activity, and thus should be considered in any wisdom of the crowd scenario, especially one involving markets.

Second, the decisions rendered must be independent, i.e., each person should not be aware of, and hence influenced by, the decisions of others. Here a question that legitimately arises is the degree to which independence of decision-making is truly an important requirement. Consider our jelly bean example above. Here it was considered important that no person estimating the number of jelly beans in the jar be aware of other people's guesses. If they were, people would presumably be influenced by prior guesses, thus affecting their independent judgment. However, it could easily be argued that if prior guesses were displayed for present guessers to see, or perhaps a running average of prior guesses was displayed, this would seemingly not detract in a large way from the accuracy of future guesses. One could even possibly argue that displaying a running average of prior guesses could improve the overall wisdom of the crowd, as future guessers benefit from the wisdom of those preceding them.

The term "social influence" in psychology refers to the concept whereby people look to the actions and behaviors of others to inform them how they themselves should behave. It is natural for a person in a crowd to look to how other members are acting to aid in deciding his own behavior. Hence, a lack of independence in decision-making would result in members of the crowd adjusting their decisions based on their observations of other people's prior decisions. If the decisions being made were influenced by the decisions of others, a herd mentality would develop, negating the diversity of opinions requirement and impairing the objectivity required for the wisdom of the crowd to manifest. Thus a lack of independence produces inferior results relative to a situation where independence is maintained.

In addition, the concept of "anchoring" or "anchor points" in psychology comes into play. Anchoring refers to the fact that the manner in which people estimate numbers is to begin with a given number or anchor point, which may or may not be relevant to the task at hand, and then adjust upward or downward from that anchor point. Numerous psychological studies have demonstrated that people generally do not sufficiently adjust from their starting anchor point. Thus in our jelly bean example the concern is that there would be insufficient adjustment from the past average of guesses, and thus the wisdom of the crowd would not truly be reflected in the result. For example, if a number of the initial guesses were either well above or below the correct answer, the psychological principles of social influence (herd mentality) and anchoring would combine to prevent sufficient deviation from these initial guesses, hence producing an incorrect answer. In a similar manner, a financial marketplace also clearly needs independent decision-making.

The third criterion is similar, if not identical, to the "diversity of opinion" criterion set out by Surowiecki. Here diversity of opinion is required such that a sufficient number of different viewpoints are expressed. This diversity of opinion helps to ensure that the full wisdom of the crowd is brought to bear on the problem at hand. Without diversity of opinion, it is quite possible that people's estimates would not be evenly distributed around the correct answer, but rather more estimates would be above the correct answer than below, or vice versa. As noted above, diversity of opinion is virtually guaranteed if the sample set is sufficiently large, whereby each person brings to the table a unique combination of knowledge, skills, experiences, and background. This diversity of opinion, assuming a sufficiently large sample set of opinions, guarantees that people's estimates will be distributed evenly around the correct answer. Certainly an adequate diversity of opinion is needed for wisdom to surface in a financial marketplace.

Fourth, the people offering opinions should not be artificially constrained by some bureaucracy or hierarchical management structure. Initially, decentralization was absent from our criteria for a financial marketplace, as this concept appeared relevant only in the context of a hierarchical structure, whereas a financial marketplace is seemingly a flattened structure. In financial markets there does not appear to be an "upper management" able to squelch the decisions of those at lower levels. However, after further consideration, lack of decentralization was deemed to be a factor, and very likely a large factor, in a financial marketplace. The lack of decentralization in a financial marketplace appears in various forms of "systemic constraints", where the term "systemic constraints" refers to overall market structural or systemic characteristics that constrain the behavior of participants and operate to skew stock prices away from correct prices. As one example, investment professionals tend to operate under a perverse incentive structure that incentivizes them to make decisions that detract from their long-term investment performance. The various systemic constraints in a financial marketplace are discussed later in Chapter 3. Regardless of form, any such lack of decentralization produces serious constraints on freedom of decision-making, with the result that many members of the crowd are not able to make decisions that they otherwise would have. This operates to reduce or even negate the input from these members, thus detracting from the wisdom of the crowd.

Fifth, the crowd members should have at least some modicum of knowledge or experience that allows them to provide an informed estimate or opinion. When the question at hand concerns the number of jelly beans in a jar, virtually everyone will have sufficient experience with the concept of volume to make an informed estimate. However, as the decision becomes more complex, an increasing number of people who lack the knowledge, education and/or experience to provide at least a moderately informed opinion may skew the results to be more "incorrect" than they otherwise would have been. It may be that the decisions of those who lack the knowledge to provide an informed opinion may be equally scattered above and below (or equally scattered around) the correct answer, and thus may average out to virtual correctness. However, this cannot be relied on. In fact, it is very possible that the lack of knowledge, education and/or experience will cause the corresponding decisions to all be skewed in a certain manner or toward a certain direction, hence detracting from crowd wisdom. Given the complexity of security selection, which if done correctly involves application of business valuation principles, knowledge should be a requirement in a financial marketplace.

Finally, the people making the decision should be rational. In other words, the decisions should be made from an intellectually sound framework, without the corrupting influences of psychological influences, biases or emotion that would impair judgment. If the members of the crowd making the estimates are biased or influenced in some way, the result will be less "ideal" or less correct than it otherwise would have been. As one example, if the people making the judgments were collectively in an extreme emotional state, the result would be much less correct. The problem with lack of rationality is that if certain biases, emotions or psychological misjudgments are present among crowd members, these will generally affect the estimates of each of the members in the same manner. Hence, the resulting influence is likely to skew the results in a single direction away from the correct result. In other words, lack of rationality is unlikely to produce answers that are evenly distributed above and below the correct answer, but instead is very likely to produce estimates that are either mostly above or mostly below the right answer. As we will see, lack of rationality has a huge effect on participants in financial markets.

Let's compare the criteria set out above with those presented by Surowiecki. Three of the criteria, independence, diversity of opinion, and decentralization, essentially mirror those proffered by Surowiecki. Aggregation is absent from the above criteria, largely because these criteria are focused on crowd requirements, not environmental requirements associated with the manner in which data / opinions are collected. Certainly aggregation is required to gather individual judgments and form a collective decision, and a financial marketplace inherently has such a mechanism. The criteria that have been added to those of Surowiecki are: 1) that the proper incentives are in place for people to provide correct answers; 5) the requirement of some element of knowledge or intelligence to provide a reasonably informed opinion; and 6) the requirement of rationality. Each of these added criteria would in fact be required in virtually any scenario for the wisdom of the crowd to be manifest. Incentives are extremely important in any area of human endeavor, as is knowledge. As we will see, while rationality can simply be presumed among participants in many group scenarios (e.g., guessing jelly beans), in many instances rationality is decidedly not present among the members of a crowd in a financial marketplace.

Let's also compare the above criteria with the elements that Francis Galton considered important in his article penned immediately after the livestock fair contest. Here after each sentence or thought we have inserted the relevant crowd wisdom criterion (*in parentheses*) to which Galton refers:

> The judgments were unbiased by passion and uninfluenced by oratory and the like (*Rationality, Independence*). The sixpenny fee deterred practical joking, and the hope of a prize and the joy of competition prompted each competitor to do his best (*Incentives, Independence, Decentralization*). The competitors included butchers and farmers, some of whom were highly expert in judging the

weight of cattle; others were probably guided by such information as they might pick up, and by their own fancies (*Knowledge*). The average competitor was probably as well fitted for making a just estimate of the dressed weight of the ox, as an average voter is of judging the merits of most political issues on which he votes (*Knowledge*), and the variety among the voters to judge justly was probably much the same in either case (*Diversity of Opinion*).[9]

In chapter 2 we discuss the manner in which modern finance has adopted the wisdom of the crowd to create the concept of "efficient markets." Chapter 3 explores the degree to which the above criteria are actually present in a crowd operating in a financial marketplace, and hence the degree to which markets are truly efficient.

2. EFFICIENT MARKET THEORY

In the stock market, academics have taken the "wisdom of the crowd" and essentially adapted it to create what is known as the "Efficient Market Theory." The Efficient Market Theory ("EMT") essentially says that the participants in the stock market are "rational actors", and information relating to businesses is widely disseminated and immediately incorporated by these rational actors into stock prices, thus producing stock prices that are always the "correct" (or nearly correct) prices. Some EMT proponents would argue that the market price of each stock reflects the current wisdom of the collective group or crowd of market participants to such an extent that it always reflects the current correct or "best" price for each stock. Others would acknowledge that according to EMT the market does not always produce correct prices, but it does produce more correct prices than any individual could provide. Regardless, according to EMT it is generally not possible, except by chance, for any one person to reliably and consistently "beat the market", i.e., to have returns better than the overall market.

Here we can think of the "correct" or "best" price of a stock as reflecting, or equivalent to, the intrinsic value of the underlying business. A short explanation of the "intrinsic value" of a business is in order. The share price of a company's stock can be multiplied by the total number of outstanding shares of the company to arrive at the company's market capitalization, this being the price the stock market is placing on the entire equity of the company. If the stock price is the correct price, the resulting market capitalization will be substantially equivalent to the intrinsic value of the business. The "intrinsic value" of the business can be considered as the value a well informed and rational private buyer would pay for the business with knowledge of all available information and conducted in an arms-length transaction, with neither side being under duress to buy or sell. When a person buys a stock of a business at the "correct" price, this can be considered as him buying a piece of the business right at the business' intrinsic value. Note that the intrinsic value of a business cannot be calculated with any degree of precision, but rather the best an investor can likely do is estimate a company's intrinsic value within a certain range. The concept of "intrinsic value" is discussed in more detail below.

There are various forms of the efficient market theory, these being the "Weak" form, the "Semistrong" form and the "Strong" form. The Weak form of EMT contends that all past market prices and data are fully reflected in securities prices. Hence, according to the Weak form, technical analysis is of little value. Of course, it can be argued that technical analysis is of little value regardless of the validity of EMT. The Semistrong form contends that all publicly available information is fully reflected in securities prices. Hence, according to the Semistrong form, fundamental analysis is of no value. Value investors obviously take issue with this form of EMT. The Strong form of EMT contends that all information, including insider information, is fully reflected in securities prices. Hence, in the Strong form, even insider information is of no value.

The Efficient Market Theory is an interesting theory. Unfortunately, the theory is simply not correct, or perhaps more generously is only partially correct. The stock market certainly does not always produce correct prices, and it also does not always produce better prices than any individual could provide. Warren Buffett said it best when he commented:

> Observing correctly that the market was *frequently* efficient, they [academics] went on to conclude incorrectly that it was *always* efficient. The difference between these two propositions is night and day.[10]

The Efficient Market Theory became widely accepted by academics in the 1970's, and a substantial number of investment professionals also fell under its spell. To this day EMT continues to hold sway in most business schools across the country. Unfortunately, once an academic theory gets accepted it seems to take forever to dislodge it. The renowned physicist Max Planck, lamenting the fact that old guard physicists clung to their theories despite much countervailing evidence that their theories were flawed, observed that: "Science advances one funeral at a time." Given the length of time that EMT has prevailed in academia, we can only hope that finance advances at least as quickly. In observing modern academics refusal to disavow EMT, despite mounting evidence of its flaws, Warren Buffett in his 1988 Berkshire Hathaway shareholder letter described the outstanding investing records of the Graham Newman Corporation, Buffett Partnership, and Berkshire Hathaway and then commented:

> Yet proponents of the theory have never seemed interested in discordant evidence of this type. True, they don't talk quite as much about their theory today as they used to. But no one, to my knowledge, has ever said he was wrong, no matter how many thousands of students he has sent forth miseducated. EMT, moreover, continues to be an integral part of the investment curriculum at major business schools. Apparently, a reluctance to recant, and thereby to demystify the priesthood, is not limited to theologians.

> Naturally the disservice done students and gullible investment professionals who have swallowed EMT has been an extraordinary service to us and other followers of Graham. In any sort of a contest - financial, mental, or physical - it's an enormous advantage to have opponents who have been taught that it's useless to even try. From a selfish point of view, Grahamites should probably endow chairs to ensure the perpetual teaching of EMT.[11]

Perhaps the best characterization of the operation of the stock market is attributed to Benjamin Graham, where he stated: "In the short run the stock market is a voting machine, and in the long run the stock market is a weighing machine."[12] Thus, in the short run stock prices are determined by the crowd's "votes" on what the correct prices should be. However, there is no intelligence test required to vote, and further, as we will see, those voting are not entirely rational, but rather are subject to various emotions, biases and errors in judgment. Thus in the short-term stock prices can deviate wildly from the correct intrinsic values of the businesses to which they correspond. In other words, stocks can often be temporarily mispriced, sometimes wildly so. However, in the long run the stock market is a weighing machine, meaning that eventually the market will price stocks correctly. One can imagine that at any instantaneous point in time the stock market operates as a voting machine, with a large number of somewhat ill-informed, sometimes wildly irrational people lined up at polling stations placing their votes on stock prices. One can also imagine the stock market operating as a slowly reacting weighing machine, whereby individual stocks are placed on the scale, and eventually, given enough time for irrationality and emotion to play itself out, the scale registers the correct value of the stock. Thus if an individual stock is currently mispriced due to irrationality, misjudgment, or systemic forces, eventually the stock market will correct this mispricing, and the stock price will ultimately return to a more correct value which better approximates the intrinsic value of the underlying business.

Another excellent characterization of the operation of the stock market comes from Howard Marks in his book *The Most Important Thing.* Here he analogizes the behavior of the stock market to a pendulum, forever moving between depression (and hence underpriced securities) and euphoria (and hence overpriced securities). The middle section of the pendulum's arc represents an intermediate position between depression and euphoria, and perhaps the location where the wisdom of the crowd actually registers to produce somewhat correct stock prices.

Unfortunately, however, the pendulum does not stay near its midpoint for very long, but rather spends most of its time swinging toward one of the two extremes. The pendulum is driven to its respective extremes largely by investor irrationality. In the words of Howard Marks:

> The mood swings of the securities markets resemble the movement of a pendulum. Although the midpoint of its arc best describes the location of the pendulum "on average," it actually spends very little of its time there. Instead, it is almost always swinging toward or away from the extremes of its arc. But whenever the pendulum is near either extreme, it is inevitable that it will move back toward the midpoint sooner or later. In fact, it is the movement toward an extreme itself that supplies the energy for the swing back.
>
> Investment markets follow a pendulum-like swing:
>
> • between euphoria and depression,
> • between celebrating positive developments and obsessing over negatives, and thus
> • between overpriced and underpriced.
>
> This oscillation is one of the most dependable features of the investment world, and investor psychology seems to spend much more time at the extremes than it does at a "happy medium."
> "FIRST QUARTER PERFORMANCE," APRIL 11, 1991[13]

Hence the reality is that the stock market is *often* efficient and stock market prices do quite often reflect the appropriate values of their underlying businesses. However, in many instances, and sometimes for lengthy periods of time, the market simply does not produce correct prices, and oftentimes individual securities are wildly mispriced. As Yogi Berra famously said: "In theory there is no difference between theory and practice, but in practice there is." The Efficient Market Theory sounds good in theory, especially in light of the wisdom of the crowd discussed earlier. However, as we will see, some of the underlying assumptions of EMT are flawed, and these flaws can be more easily perceived when analyzing the various criteria discussed above for the "wisdom of the crowd" to apply.

To illustrate the inefficiency of markets, examine the stock pages of the local newspaper, select virtually any large cap stock, and then consider the variation between the 52-week high and the 52-week low of that stock. You will find that the vast majority of large cap stocks have a fairly large variation between their 52-week high and 52-week low, and some will have a variation of 100% or more. Of course we know that the intrinsic values of these companies did not change nearly this much over the course of one year. This is merely a reflection of the market's inefficiency in placing prices on businesses. If all businesses were required to change hands only by negotiated transactions between private buyers and sellers, the prices would be much more predictably accurate, and there would not be such huge swings in valuation of a company over the course of a year. For example, consider a situation where a particular buyer was negotiating with a seller to purchase a business. If the negotiation over the price continued for 6 – 9 months, it would be almost unimaginable to think that the price would change by 30% or more during this time, barring some huge fundamental change in the business itself. But this change in valuation happens in markets all the time. If all businesses were bought and sold in private transactions, investors would not be able to routinely beat the market because the prices would for the most part be rationally determined. The above example provides evidence of market inefficiency during normal years. Of course, during times of extreme fear and greed, the mispricings that occur are often of an extreme nature, and market inefficiency is much more clearly on display.

Modern finance teaches that the great number of supposedly rational participants providing input on stock prices is what produces correct prices. In other words, crowd wisdom is at work in the stock market, producing correct prices. The great irony here is the mere fact that stocks are traded by a great number of participants on a large, liquid market exchange is largely what produces such large discrepancies between price and value. In other words, the fact that a large number of decidedly irrational participants are voting on stock prices, combined with the incredible liquidity of the market, is actually what produces market inefficiency. The liquidity aspect of markets as a contributing factor to market inefficiency cannot be overstated. A privately negotiated transaction between a buyer and a seller requires much time and effort, and is not entered into lightly. In contrast, in the stock market a piece of a business can be sold in a second with the mere click of a button. The ease with which pieces of a business can be bought and sold in the stock market provides a huge temptation for irrational participants to make thoughtless and often emotional buy and sell decisions that are divorced from reality.

Whenever EMT proponents are confronted with arguments or evidence that the market is not efficient, they tend to counter this reality by pointing to the fact that only a very small percentage of participants consistently beat the market over any length of time. This, they say, is proof that the market is efficient, i.e., efficient at least in the sense that it produces better answers than the vast majority of individual participants can provide. Certainly it is disconcerting to consider the relatively poor records that most professional (and individual) participants have relative to the overall market. However, as we will see, the poor investment performance of the majority of the market crowd is largely due to irrationality, incorrect incentives, various systemic constraints (mostly short-term mindsets and overdiversification), and herd mentality present in the market. A financial marketplace by its very nature is specifically adapted to produce incorrect / irrational behavior, and hence given this it is surprising that the market is as efficient as it is. However, if an investor is able to maintain a long-term investment horizon and avoid the irrationality and herd mentality that is so prevalent in the market, and if he uses a fundamental value-based approach in selecting a focused portfolio of investments, he has much better odds of beating the market. In other words, if an investor harkens from the intellectual village of Graham and Doddsville, or Buffettville, he is much more likely to consistently and reliably beat the market averages than if he hails from Wall Street. In addition, if the investor is knowledgeable regarding the powerful forces of crowd wisdom, and in particular the limitations of crowd wisdom in financial markets, he will be better positioned to become a successful investor.

We will finish this chapter with a joke that is often told by value investors and finance professors alike. The joke goes like this:

> A finance professor and a student are walking down a street. The student notices a $100 bill lying on the pavement and leans down to pick it up. The finance professor immediately intervenes and says, "Don't bother; all markets are completely efficient. If that were a real $100 bill lying there, somebody would have already picked it up."

Value investors complete this joke with the skeptical student picking up the $100 bill and happily pocketing the money. The lesson here is that the student, who has not yet been corrupted with false theories about efficient markets, and who remains skeptical of both Wall Street professionals and learned professors, is still able to believe his own eyes when he spots inefficiencies in the market, and is able to profit from them.

Finance professors, on the other hand, complete this joke in a very different manner which holds true to their theory of efficient markets. A popular finance text, after reciting the above joke, goes on to say:

This joke invariably generates much laughter because it makes fun of the principle of no arbitrage in competitive markets. But once the laughter dies down, the professor then asks whether anyone has ever *actually* found a real $100 bill lying on the pavement. The ensuing silence is the real lesson behind the joke.

This joke sums up the point of focusing on markets in which no arbitrage opportunities exist. Free $100 bills lying on the pavement, like arbitrage opportunities, are extremely rare for two reasons: (1) Because $100 is a large amount of money, people are especially careful not to lose it, and (2) in the rare event when someone does inadvertently drop $100, the likelihood of your finding it before someone else does is extremely small.[14]

The flaw in the finance professor's thinking is that he fails to account for the operation of liquid markets, and especially irrational crowd behavior in those markets, in creating these "arbitrage opportunities", the proverbial $100 bills lying on the sidewalk. True, there are not many $100 bills lying on the literal sidewalks for people to snatch up, but here there is no highly liquid market, crowd behavior and/or systemic irrationality to create such opportunities. As we will see, due to the inherent irrationality and herd behavior of the crowd at play in a financial marketplace, markets are specifically adapted to create these mispricings. Thus there will be periods of time in a market when emotions are running high and there will literally be $100 bills, and in fact million dollar bills, strewn about on the sidewalks, and the investor won't be able to pick them up fast enough. In our own experience, there have been times (e.g., 2009 and 2011) when the million dollar bills were everywhere, and we were lamenting the fact that we did not have enough capital to seize all of the "arbitrage opportunities" the supposedly efficient market was presenting to us.

3. THE FOOLISHNESS OF THE CROWD

The wisdom of the crowd is a powerful force. When a large number of people apply their judgment to a particular estimate or result, and certain criteria are met, the collective judgment of the crowd produces a very good result, much better than any single member of the crowd and better than any expert. However, the stock market often produces incorrect results, sometimes very large mispricings. These mispricings – these inefficiencies in the market – are due to a lack of crowd wisdom that we call the "Foolishness of the Crowd." This raises the following questions: Given the large number of people voting on stock prices, why doesn't the "wisdom of the crowd" apply to the stock market at all times? How can such large discrepancies between price and value arise? Why doesn't crowd wisdom dictate correct stock prices all of the time?

To answer these questions, let's go back and analyze the criteria we developed in Chapter 1 for the wisdom of the crowd to apply. These criteria are as follows:

1. Incentives: the proper incentives are in place for people to provide the correct answer

2. Independence: the decisions are independent – each person is not aware of or affected by the decisions of others.

3. Diversity of Opinion: the people have sufficiently different backgrounds, education, experience, and/or knowledge such that a diversity of opinion is provided.

4. Decentralization: the people are able to make their decisions without bureaucratic or systemic constraints.

5. Knowledge: the people generally have at least a modicum of knowledge or experience that allows them to provide some type of informed estimate or opinion.

6. Rationality: the people making the decisions think in a rational manner in formulating their opinions.

Let's analyze each of these criteria in turn. At the outset we note that many of the various facets of human behavior discussed below do not fit neatly just into individual ones of the above categories, but rather fall within a number of the above criteria. Thus the different behavioral aspects are principally described in what is deemed to be the most relevant criteria category, and for the sake of completeness they are also mentioned in related categories as well. Hence the discussion below errs on the side of comprehensiveness, at the expense of some inevitable overlap in content.

1. Incentives

The first requirement is that the people have the appropriate or proper incentives to provide the correct answer. At first blush this requirement does not even seem to be needed. Surely all market participants, whether they be investor or speculator, amateur or professional, have the incentive to maximize their overall returns in the stock market. The way to achieve optimal profits would of course be to accurately estimate the future course of stock prices, and buy and sell stocks accordingly. "What other incentive could market participants possible have?" one might ask.

Individual (nonprofessional) market participants seem to have the proper incentive – to produce the best financial results possible. For example, there are no apparent ulterior motives that would detract from this incentive. Individual participants are not paid by others to select stocks, and thus there is no alternative form of income that would compete in terms of relative importance with stock market returns. In addition, individuals largely select stocks in obscurity, and thus their stock selection is not affected by how others might view their portfolio. If they make a poor stock purchase, perhaps only their spouse or a few friends will know of it. In summary, individual investors are "compensated" solely based on their personal market returns, and they are not really accountable to anyone else but themselves. Thus an individual's incentive is relatively straightforward – do the best job he can to maximize his overall returns. The best way to maximize returns in the stock market would seemingly be to correctly estimate the future course of stock prices.

For professional money managers, however, the role of incentives is somewhat more complex. In fact, the reality is that professionals have a number of different, sometimes competing incentives to contend with. Many of these incentives tend to cause a deviation from the goal of providing the best possible investment decisions. In financial markets, as is true in many areas of human endeavor, perhaps the most important overriding incentive for professional managers is to maximize personal financial gain. This is not the same goal as either maximizing stock market returns or correctly estimating stock prices. Many professional money managers are paid largely or exclusively based on assets under management (AUM) or their contribution thereto. Thus a key incentive for many professional money managers is client gathering and retention, i.e., to promote fund deposits and limit withdrawals in order to maximize AUM. For many professionals their compensation structure is designed to incentivize sales – new client origination – much more than fund performance.

Another way to maximize AUM is to reduce investor angst regarding fund performance. As discussed further below, people tend to handle uncertainty very poorly, and stock price volatility is one type of uncertainty that many market participants find especially troubling. Thus, many professional managers design portfolios explicitly to minimize volatility, at the expense of overall returns. A stock portfolio designed at least partly to minimize volatility will generally not be optimized to correctly predict and take advantage of stock mispricings. A paper titled "Best Ideas" reported research results indicating that the highest conviction stock selections of active money managers produced the best returns (highest alpha), and that the selections with lesser conviction did not exhibit any outperformance (no alpha). In discussing the reasons why many active managers over-diversify their portfolios and hence reduce their performance, the authors state:

> Our findings suggest that while the typical manager has a small number of good investment ideas that provide positive alpha in expectation, the remaining ideas in the typical managed portfolio add no alpha at all. Managers have understandable incentives to include these zero-alpha positions. Without them, the portfolio would contain only a few names, leading to increased volatility, price impact, illiquidity, and regulatory/litigation risk. Adding additional stocks to the portfolio can not only reduce volatility but also increase portfolio Sharpe ratio. Perhaps most important, adding names enables the manager to take in more assets, and thus draw greater management fees. But while the manager gains from diversifying the portfolio, it is likely that typical investors are made worse off.[15]

Another related and very important way that professional managers attempt to maximize personal gain, and as a byproduct maintain job security, is the simple desire to avoid looking foolish. For example, most professionals would not consider purchasing a stock that was considered "unusual" for fear of looking foolish if the investment turned out poorly. They fear that they would lose business if they stood too far apart from the crowd. As the famed economist John Maynard Keynes noted: "Worldly wisdom teaches that it is better for reputation to fail conventionally than to succeed unconventionally."[16] In other words, most professional money managers would rather stick to conventional stock selection, purchasing stocks that other professionals are buying, even with the knowledge that this will produce mediocre results, rather than risk purchasing unconventional stocks that would promise a greater possibility of outperformance, due to the small chance of failure and embarrassment. If a professional manager selects Johnson & Johnson for his portfolio, and J&J does poorly, then the professional manager can blame J&J ("What is wrong with J&J these days?"), knowing that most of the professional herd will also have selected this stock and will sympathize and commiserate with his plight. However, if the professional selects a less conventional stock, one not widely followed by analysts or widely held among the professional community, and the stock does poorly, the professional will be alone in his failure, and will not be able to point to convention as a defense.

In his book *One Up on Wall Street*, Peter Lynch provided some insight on the role of client retention and job security in professional stock purchasing decisions:

> Whoever imagines that the average Wall Street professional is looking for reasons to buy exciting stocks hasn't spent much time on Wall Street. The fund manager most likely is looking for reasons *not* to buy exciting stocks, so that he can offer the proper excuses if those exciting stocks happen to go up. 'It was too small for me to buy' heads a long list, followed by 'there was no track record,' 'it was in a non-growth industry,'' unproven management,' 'the employees belong to a union,' and 'the competition will kill them,' . . . .

> With survival at stake, it's the rare professional who has the guts to traffic in an [unknown stock]. In fact, between the chance of making an unusually large profit on an unknown company and the assurance of losing only a small amount on an established company, the normal mutual-fund manager, pension-fund manager, or corporate-portfolio manager would jump at the latter. Success is one thing, but it's more important not to look bad if you fail.[17]

If a professional selects a stock portfolio that is markedly different than his peers, then his performance will also likely be different, in either a good or bad way. Bad performance is generally punished more harshly than good performance is rewarded. Thus the incentive in professional stock selection is much more toward conformity with peers than outperformance. Thus for many, perhaps most, professionals the incentive structure is not entirely aligned with producing the best investment decisions possible. Instead, many such decisions are made for the purpose of maximizing personal compensation or maintaining job security.

Of course one way for a professional money manager to attract and keep clients is to attain outsized returns – to provide good results to his clients – and in this he has the proper incentive to provide correct stock market decisions. Relatively few money managers seem to accomplish this on a regular basis, however, and it is not clear how important of a role this incentive plays vs. the other incentives discussed above.

In addition, due to the fact that the vast majority of professionals are graded on a very frequent basis, short-term thinking is another manifestation of the professional's incentive structure. This topic is discussed below in the section on Decentralization.

2. Independence

The second requirement is that the decisions of the members of the crowd are independent, i.e., each person is not aware of the decisions of others. In a financial marketplace such as the stock market, this requirement is clearly not met. Current stock prices are published 24 hours a day, seven days a week, for all the world to see. Prices are updated instantaneously not only during regular trading hours, but in after-hours trading as well. Stock prices essentially represent an average of everyone's votes on what current stock prices should be. Thus everyone who purchases stocks is acutely aware of what the remainder of the crowd believes the correct price to be. Many would-be investors have stock prices constantly scrolling across their computer screens, lest they miss any movement in prices.

3. THE FOOLISHNESS OF THE CROWD

A more recent development in stock price information overload is television coverage of the financial markets. A number of cable TV channels are devoted to financial news, with celebrity commentators pontificating on stocks and providing mostly worthless stock recommendations to the masses. In addition, numerous "talking heads" are present in the media discussing stocks and stock prices on a daily basis. This television onslaught brings the herd-like mentality of the crowd into everyone's living room, making it extremely difficult for viewers to think and act independently, to stand apart from the crowd. In fact, it would seem difficult for a person to isolate himself from stock price information, as market participants are constantly bombarded with such information from many different sources. Perhaps more damaging, this media coverage creates the false impression that investing is easy and that the focus should be on short-term results. Nothing could be more detrimental to individual investor performance.

The most impactful role of the media in a financial marketplace arises from their incentive to fan the flames of passion during periods of fear and greed. Like any business, the primary goal of a media company is to maximize profits. This is accomplished largely through advertising revenue, which in turn is based on the number of eyeballs viewing its content. Hence any media company reporting on financial events has a tremendous built-in incentive to play to the passions of the crowd, to portray every economic hiccup as a full grown economic crisis and to portray companies with new products as must-win story stocks promising instant wealth. In doing so, financial media companies hope to gain viewership and hence increase their advertising revenue. The principal by-product of this is increased irrationality, increased fear and greed, on the part of the crowd.

Experimental research conducted at a science and technology university in Zurich (ETH Zurich) has shown that the power of "social proof" or "social influence" – the tendency of people to conform to the actions of others – undermines the wisdom of the crowd effect.[18] This experimental research demonstrated that even mild forms of social influence undermine the wisdom of the crowd in simple estimation tasks. The research involved experiments where a number of subjects were asked to estimate the answers to factual questions, and then were given the chance to reconsider their answers after being provided an average of the answers from the other respondents. The experiment also included a control group that did not receive information on other subject's responses. The conclusion of these experiments was that the collective answers from the subject's initial estimations were "wise", i.e., the average of their answers produced generally correct decisions. However, once information of other subject's responses was introduced, the diversity of opinions narrowed sufficiently that the wisdom of the crowd was "undermined."

This research, published in the Proceedings of the National Academy of Sciences (PNAS) concluded as follows:

> Although groups are initially "wise," knowledge about estimates of others narrows the diversity of opinions to such an extent that it undermines the wisdom of crowd effect in three different ways. The "social influence effect" diminishes the diversity of the crowd without improvements of its collective error. The "range reduction effect" moves the position of the truth to peripheral regions of the range of estimates so that the crowd becomes less reliable in providing expertise for external observers. The "confidence effect" boosts individuals' confidence after convergence of their estimates despite lack of improved accuracy.[19]

Therefore the conclusion of this research was that when members of the crowd are aware of the viewpoints and decisions of others, the diversity of their decisions is reduced. More specifically, they tend to adjust their views to better correspond with the views of others, and thus their decisions become more like one another, causing a corresponding reduction in the diversity of estimates produced. This conformity does not actually improve the accuracy of the crowd, but rather detracts from it. Thus, the resulting range of estimates from the "tainted" crowd members moves away from the correct answer. Thus, individuals in a group modify their own viewpoints based on the judgments of others to the extent that the resulting average of their views is further from the correct answer than it otherwise would have been.

One commentator on this research noted:

> Imagine that a government tries to use the wisdom of crowds, assembling a group and surveying their opinions, hoping to get a range of views and some idea of how much consensus there is on some topic. You would hope that, if the crowd's estimate was NOT accurate, this lack of accuracy would be reflected in a wide range of estimates from the individuals -- the wide range would signal a lack of unanimity and confidence. A truly bad outcome would be a crowd that at once gives a very inaccurate estimate and does so with a narrow range of opinion differences, signaling apparent strong certainty in the result. But this is precisely what the research found -- in the social influence conditions, the individuals' estimates didn't "bracket" the true answer, with some being higher and others lower. Rather, the group narrowed the range of their views so strongly that the truth tended to reside outside of the group's range . . . .[20]

Unfortunately, due to the effects of social influence, stock market participants often suffer from this "truly bad outcome." Not only is the judgment of the investing crowd largely inaccurate, but the consensus of opinions falls within an unduly narrow range, conveying a false sense of certainty in the result. Hence another effect of social influence on crowd behavior determined by this research was an increase in confidence among individual members of the crowd. We know from behavioral psychology that people generally suffer from "overconfidence bias" – they innately tend to be overconfident in their own knowledge, abilities, and judgments. People thus tend to have greater confidence in their own judgments than warranted by the accuracy of their judgments. When an individual makes an estimate with knowledge of other people's estimates, his inherent overconfidence bias in the correctness of his own estimate increases – his normal overconfidence is actually magnified. This increase in overconfidence comes from two different sources: 1) the knowledge that the estimate he is initially providing is consistent with prior estimates of the crowd; and 2) subsequent observations that the crowd, as indicated by stock prices, continues to agree with his estimate. Overconfidence bias, in and of itself, is undesirable as it detracts from objective analysis and prevents people from reconsidering their decisions. The increase in overconfidence caused by social influence produces an even greater lack of objectivity.

Thus social influence has a very pernicious effect on crowd wisdom, not only causing the crowd as a whole to produce incorrect answers, but also causing individual members of the crowd to have a large amount of undue confidence in the result. It is relatively easy to imagine the effect on stock market participants as they place buy and sell orders with current stock prices – the collective judgment of the financial crowd – scrolling across their computer screens. They not only adjust their buy and sell orders based on the current crowd consensus, contributing to incorrect market prices, but having placed their order they have unwarranted confidence in the correctness of their action. Subsequent market price movements, tainted by the effects of social influence, tend to confirm their prior decisions, creating even more overconfidence as the crowd seemingly justifies their prior decisions. As events unfold which should cause participants to reevaluate their decisions, their overconfidence prevents them from doing so. Instead they find comfort in being part of the herd, knowing that their votes on stock prices conform to the judgment of the market as a whole. Hence, ironically, social influence not only contributes to the initial establishment of incorrect stock prices, but in addition actually contributes to the persistence of these incorrect prices due to a collective overconfidence in the result.

It seems irrefutable that the lack of independence among market participants is a serious stumbling block to achieving a wisdom of the crowd effect, primarily due to the effects of herd mentality, especially when emotions are running high. However, one might think that professional investors, with their supposedly superior knowledge, training and experience, should be above the effects of this herd mentality. Certainly professional investors, most of whom have attended business school and many having received training and experience with a venerable investment firm, would have confidence in their own judgment and not fall under the influence of the herd. Nothing could be further from the truth. Professional investors suffer from their own particular constraints, including constant demands for short-term results, size limitations, and portfolio restrictions (all discussed further below). But even more than that, professional investors by and large suffer from their own social influences or herd mentality, referred to by Warren Buffett as the "institutional imperative." Buffett coined the term "institutional imperative" to refer to actions on the part of businessmen and investment managers to mindlessly imitate the behavior of their peers, no matter how foolish.

One professional mutual fund manager who managed to overcome this professional herd mentality was Peter Lynch. In *One Up on Wall Street* Lynch provided a scathing assessment of the groupthink and "camp-following" of professional investors. After describing a few of the great value investors such as John Templeton and Warren Buffett, Lynch noted:

> These notable exceptions are entirely outnumbered by the run-of-the-mill fund managers, dull fund managers, comatose fund managers, sycophantic fund

managers, timid fund managers, plus other assorted camp followers, fuddy-duddies, and copycats hemmed in by the rules.

Under the current system, a stock isn't truly attractive until a number of large institutions have recognized its suitability and an equal number of respected Wall Street analysts (the researchers who track the various industries and companies) have put it on the recommended list. With so many people waiting for others to make the first move, it's amazing that anything gets bought.[21]

The result of this is the phenomenon whereby investment managers largely buy the same securities so that their portfolios are not markedly different from anyone else's. For the sake of completeness, the all-important incentive for professionals to maximize personal income and maintain job security (previously discussed) produces an even greater amount of conformity in investment portfolios.

Professional money managers seem to experience a stronger pull from social influence (a much stronger sense of herd mentality) than individual non-professionals. As noted above, individuals largely select stocks in obscurity and are not really accountable to anyone else but themselves. Professionals, on the other hand, are largely immersed in a culture of continual stock selection judgment - they are judged on their stock picks by both their clients and their peers on a regular, and short-term, basis. For a professional money manager, the idea of standing apart from the crowd and being wrong is quite painful, and the censure from his firm and his client can be quite severe. To be sure, professionals have techniques to attempt to hide their mistakes from their bosses, clients and peers. In the professional management business, indiscriminate selling of current losers prior to the end of a reporting period is called "burying the evidence." Hand in hand with "burying the evidence" is the idea of "window dressing" the portfolio – purchasing stocks that have recently done well to give the appearance that the professional is making wise investment decisions. Thus when the professional investor's client reviews the portfolio, he will not see the laggards and mistakes, but rather see companies who have had a recent run-up in stock price (even though the fund did not benefit from this run-up). However, these techniques are by no means foolproof, and thus conformity is the best line of defense against the appearance of looking foolish.

3. Diversity of Opinion

The third requirement is that the people generally have sufficiently different backgrounds, education, experience, and/or knowledge such that a diversity of opinion is provided. This requirement is almost certainly met. At any given time between 50% to 70% of Americans participate in the stock market in some form, either by holding individual stocks, stock mutual funds, or stocks in their 401k's.[22] There are also a large number of international participants in the U.S. stock market. Every day 1.5 to 2.5 billion shares trade hands on the New York Stock Exchange. Moreover, the participants in the stock market come from all walks of life, from every geographic corner of the United States and much of the world, from many different income levels, and from many different experience levels, from the novice to the experienced professional. Put simply, there is an extremely wide diversity of people who cast votes in the stock market, so much so that virtually every type of viewpoint and stock selection methodology is represented many times over. Clearly there is sufficient diversity of opinion in the stock market for the wisdom of the crowd to apply.

However, in the section on independence above we discussed the manner in which social influence (lack of independence) impairs diversity of opinion. Due to the crowd behavior at play in a financial marketplace, the tendency of people to act in a herd-like manner critically impacts the presence of diversity in the marketplace. This is especially the case when emotions are running high, due to either a state of euphoric greed or depressive anxiety and fear. The conformity of action caused by stock market excesses of greed and fear tends to seriously reduce the required diversity of opinion required for the wisdom of the crowd. During these times market participants tend to strongly conform to the actions of the herd. Thus as the stock market pendulum swings incessantly between periods of fear and greed, near the midpoint of these cycles there is usually sufficient diversity of opinion for the crowd to produce wisdom. However, near the endpoints, as the psychological pendulum nears its terminus in either direction, herd behavior is rampant, and diversity of opinion is all but lost. Thus perhaps the best that can be said on this subject is that quite often diversity of opinion is certainly present in the market, but during times of extreme emotion, of extreme fear or greed, this diversity largely disappears.

4. Decentralization

The fourth requirement is decentralization – the notion that the people are able to make their decisions without being artificially constrained by a hierarchical bureaucracy or other systemic constraints. In the context of a financial marketplace, the concept of decentralization has been adapted to apply to several "systemic constraints" – systemic or institutional factors that inhibit or constrain decision-making. These factors include the short-term results mindset and grading system of Wall Street, the size constraints of large institutional funds, the portfolio restrictions imposed by most mutual funds, and the rise of indexation as an investment vehicle and its influence on stock prices. Let's examine these in turn. Note that herd mentality could easily have fallen here in the decentralization category (or perhaps more logically the irrationality category), but was already described above in the section on independence. Also note that this list of systemic constraints is by no means exhaustive – there are likely many others not mentioned here.

The first example of a systemic constraint on decision-making is Wall Street's institutional emphasis on short-term trading results over long-term wealth generation. Although this short-term mindset among professional money managers could easily be classified as a form of irrationality, or a result of misplaced incentives, it is included here due to its institutional nature. For professional money managers, there is tremendous pressure from the Wall Street investment culture, and usually also from their overseers and clients, to focus on the short term. In fact, the incentives heavily emphasize short-term performance, i.e., in any given quarter the professional is expected to do well, and not underperform. This emphasis primarily manifests itself in the grading system employed by Wall Street firms and their clients, whereby professional money managers are often graded on a quarterly, or even more frequent, basis. It's almost as if an invisible bureaucracy existed on Wall Street which mandated that stock selection be based on whether the stock price is likely to increase over the next few weeks or months. Thus the mentality of Wall Street overall, including both investment firms and clients, places a heavy focus on short-term thinking and a short-term outlook in stock selection.

As Henry Blodget, former head of global Internet research at Merrill Lynch, once commented:

> If you talk to a lot of investment managers, the practical reality is they're thinking about the next week, possibly the next month or quarter. There isn't a time horizon; it's how are you doing *now*, relative to your competitors. You really only have ninety days to be right, and if you're wrong within ninety days, your clients begin to fire you.

And as Seth Klarman commented in his excellent preface to the 6th Edition of Graham and Dodd's Security Analysis:

> Nearly all money managers today, including some hapless value managers, are forced by the (real or imagined) performance pressures of the investment business to have an absurdly short investment horizon, sometimes as brief as a calendar quarter, month, or less.[23]

Thus, even where individual stock analysts may desire to select investments based on a long-term perspective (and it seems there are precious few of these), they are graded on a short-term basis, generally on a quarterly basis. Hence, for those managers who would desire to more wisely invest with a long-term horizon in mind, they are effectively prevented, or at least heavily discouraged, from doing so. This systemic mindset produces a large constraint on stock selection, and in reality greatly limits the long-term returns of professional money managers.

Recall in Chapter 2 the discussion of Ben Graham's characterization of the stock market as a voting machine in the short run, where in the short term stock prices are largely unpredictable due to the irrational votes of market participants. Thus, even though professional managers may have an edge over the average individual investor in the amount of raw information at their disposal, their short-term investment horizon forces them to deal with much more randomness and unpredictability in stock prices. Trying to beat a market benchmark on a quarter-by-quarter basis is extremely difficult, and is more often the result of luck than skill. Very few money managers are able to repeatedly outperform the indexes with such a short-term mindset. This is a significant factor as to why such a large percentage of professional money managers do not beat the S&P 500 index.

In fact, one can argue that the greatest advantage that the individual investor has over professionals is the ability to think and act based on a long-term perspective. For example, if a particular stock is deemed to be undervalued, but there is no apparent near term catalyst that would increase the stock price in the short term, most professional money managers would shy away from investing in the stock. Individual investors can buy stocks based on value considerations, knowing they have the ability to wait a period of years for the market to validate their reasoning, i.e., they can wait for the "weighing machine" personality of the market to take effect. Unfortunately, many individual market participants fail to take advantage of this edge over the professional class, i.e., many individual participants have a short-term mindset that rivals the professionals. Alas, the psychological need to "get rich quick" is difficult to overcome.

Size constraints form a second example of a systemic constraint on stock selection. As the amount of money flowing into large, professionally managed funds has increased, the size of these large funds has constrained the types of investments open to them. In addition, many funds are constrained by rules that require investments to have at least a minimum market capitalization. Further, most indexes are created with the knowledge (or hope) that a large amount of money will be committed to these indexes, and hence liquidity of the index is paramount. Accordingly, large cap stocks are generally the only choice for large index funds, and the same large cap stocks tend to appear over and over in different large indexes. Hence the reality is that most large funds, whether indexed or not, are simply too large in size to buy small-cap or even some mid-cap stocks. Stated another way, small-cap and mid-cap stocks often simply do not have a sufficiently large market capitalization to support an investment by a large fund. If a large fund were to attempt to take a position in a small-cap stock, it would likely have to buy a large percentage of the stock to take any type of meaningful position. For example, in order for a large fund to buy a position in a small-cap company large enough to make a difference in the fund's performance, the fund would likely have to buy 20% or more of the company. However, the Securities and Exchange Commission (SEC) places onerous regulations on mutual funds that make it difficult for funds to establish positions of this size. Hence certain large cap stocks tend to be overbought, especially when a rising pool of money is flowing into mutual funds. Similarly, stocks that are not part of established indexes and stocks too small to appear in large professionally managed funds tend to be under-bought, creating opportunities for the investor.

In fact, ironically enough, the market capitalization rules imposed on most funds limit their ability to buy shares in small companies when they are a bargain. Instead, these funds are relegated to only purchasing such companies until after there has been a large run-up in stock price sufficient to raise the company's market capitalization over the fund's purchase threshold. Consider the example of a mutual fund with a market-capitalization rule which dictates that the fund cannot own the stock of a company less than $100 million in size. Now assume a company with 20 million shares outstanding selling for $1.50 per share. Such a company has a market cap of $30 million and hence must be avoided by the fund. Only after the stock price has quadrupled to 6$ per share is the company suitable for investment.[24]

Another area where size constraints create price distortions is in the area of spin-offs. A spin-off involves a company splitting off or separating a section of itself, e.g., a subsidiary, in order to create a new independent business. Often the spinoff company is small enough in size that many funds that own the parent company are forced to immediately sell their interests in the spinoff company. This causes an indiscriminate selling of the spinoff company's stock, driving down the spinoff company's stock price without regard to value considerations.

Portfolio constraints in mutual funds are another example of a systemic constraint on stock selection. In addition to constraints on the size of companies that can be purchased, most funds also suffer from constraints on the *type* of companies they can buy. The fund universe has been partitioned into numerous different categories, such as small cap, mid cap, large cap, growth, value, blended, sector funds, domestic funds, global funds and so many others that fund managers are seriously constrained by their fund itself. Many mutual funds these days are so specialized that the investment policy of the fund acts as a serious restriction on what can be purchased. Thus in the unlikely event (due to his need for conformity) that a fund manager is able to identify a bargain security that he desires to purchase, more often than not the fund's investment policy prevents him from doing so. In addition, many institutions place additional limitations on the stocks that can be purchased by a fund, e.g., some institutions prohibit the purchase of stocks in "non-growth" industries, stocks which do not pay dividends, or investment in specific industries such as utilities, energy, etc.

A fourth example of a systemic constraint is the rise of indexation, including both index mutual funds and Exchange Traded Funds (ETF's). ETF's are investment funds that hold assets such as stocks or bonds and which trade like a stock on a stock exchange. The great majority of ETF's track a stock or bond index. The growth of assets under management (AUM) in ETF's is staggering, growing from a mere $800 million in AUM in equity ETF's in 1993 to over $1 trillion of AUM by the end of 2010. Index mutual funds and ETF's that track an index are collectively referred to here as index funds for convenience.

The vast amount of money placed in index funds has created almost a dual class of stocks, those that are present in an index and those that are not. Stocks that compose an index are purchased when an investor chooses to allocate his money to the relevant index fund. In this case, the stocks that make up the index are purchased without any regard to their underlying value. Similarly, when an investor chooses to sell his share of an index fund, the stocks composing the index are indiscriminately sold, again without regard to their underlying value. In addition, with any index there will be stocks with different valuation metrics that compose the index. However, the presence of these stocks in the index means that they will all be bought and sold together. Thus a company which is a poor value proposition, but which is present in a popular index, will essentially have its price supported by the other members of the index. In other words, when an investor buys into the index, he is committed to buy these poor value stocks along with every other member of the index. This all or nothing approach in the buying and selling of stocks in popular indexes is a form of centralization – stocks composing an index are now coupled, joined at the hip, and are largely bought and sold together, even though they may have very different valuation metrics.

Further, people tend to pile money into funds during bull markets, i.e., during periods of rising stock prices, thus requiring the professional to allocate this additional money to stocks during periods of high stock prices. Conversely, they tend to withdraw money from funds during bear markets, i.e., during periods of falling stock prices, thus requiring the professional to liquidate positions during periods of low stock prices. Thus the stocks composing an index, and in addition the small universe of large cap stocks that compose most large mutual funds, are generally bought and sold en masse at precisely the wrong times. This operates to distort the prices of stocks composing the popular indices, inflating them during bull markets and hastening their demise in bear markets.

Another indexation-related systemic constraint on stock selection is the manner in which the weightings of the various stock indexes are calculated. Traditionally, index funds were full capitalization weighted indices, also referred to as full market value weighted indices, meaning that the components (companies) of the stock market index were weighted according to the total market value of their outstanding shares. As the stock price of an individual stock in the index changed, the impact of that stock price change was proportional to the overall market value of the respective company. The key here was that, for each company making up the index, all of the company's outstanding shares were taken into account in determining the weight of that company in the index. Thus, for example, shares that were held by company insiders and governmental entities were considered in the weighting calculation.

In 2005, many of the indexes, including the S&P 500, transitioned to a free-float weighted version of capitalization weighting. In the free-float weighting method, a float factor is assigned to each stock to account for the proportion of outstanding shares that are held by the general public. This float factor excludes "closely held" shares owned by the government or insiders. Thus, for example, if a company had an owner-operator that owned 20% of the outstanding shares of the company, with the remaining 80% of the shares held by the general public, only this 80% of the shares would be considered in its weighting in the index. This change in the manner in which capitalization weighting is calculated seems innocuous enough. In fact, S&P commented at the time of the transition that "We looked at the academic and theoretical basis for indexing, but found no arguments for or against float adjustment."[25]

However, the change from a full capitalization weighted calculation to a free-float weighted calculation has some unintended consequences. In particular, the free-float weighted calculation tends to reduce the contribution of companies with large insider ownership, for example companies run by "owner-operators." The term "owner-operator" refers to a company that is managed by a founder / owner, who is a large shareholder of the company, as opposed to a company run by an "agent operator", a manager hired to run the company who is not a founder and/or who has a relatively small equity stake in the company (except for the large stock options he routinely grants himself). A strong case can be made that companies run by owner operators make better business and capital allocation decisions than do companies run by outside management. As Horizon Research Group noted in their essay "The Owner-Operator Company: A Superior Business Model":

> At owner-operator companies, decisions are made by a principal or owner, as opposed to an agent or hired manager. For agent-operator companies, the typical hired CEO cannot ignore career issues and the related need to manage short-term reactive expectations of shareholders and analysts. Agent-operators also must abide by arbitrarily set benchmarks such as market share or revenue growth. Contrarily, judgments at owner-operator companies are largely based on long-term return-on-capital considerations. They also demonstrate heightened awareness of business and balance sheet risk.[26]

In short, owner-operators have a strong owner orientation, meaning that they are primarily focused on long-term wealth creation as opposed to short-term profits. Owner-operators typically also have more of a value investor's mindset when it comes to capital allocation. They typically are ready to act decisively and make large investments during times of financial distress.

Owner-operator companies have generally outperformed agent-operator companies, and hence their presence in an index has generally increased the overall performance of the index. For example, consider Walmart under the leadership of Sam Walton, Microsoft under the leadership of Bill Gates, etc. During these owner-operator periods each of these companies experienced exceptional growth and stock price performance. Much of the exceptional growth of these companies during the owner-operator period was due to the fact that a company will naturally experience much greater growth from its founding up to maturity. In addition, at least some of this exceptional growth is without doubt due to the fact that the company was being better managed by the owner-operator. Regardless, the fact remains that during the owner-operator management period companies will generally experience greater share price growth than during agent operator periods.

Prior to the change to a free-float based index weighting, owner-operator companies were fully represented in the index to which they belonged, i.e., all of the shares of the owner-operator company were considered in that company's weighting within the index, including the shares owned by their founders (owner-operators). For example, all of Bill Gates shares of Microsoft were considered when calculating Microsoft's weighting in the index. However, with free-float based index weighting, all of the shares held by the owner of the company (all closely held shares) are now excluded from the weighting calculation. Thus, whereas history would indicate that owner-operator companies have on a relative basis contributed the most to an index fund's performance, with free-float based index weighting owner-operator companies now constitute a smaller contribution to the index than they used to. Owners of index funds, in the interests of fund performance, should want owner-operator companies to contribute to its constituent index fund to the maximum extent possible. However, this change in capitalization weighting is very likely to decrease index fund performance from what it otherwise would have been.

The free-float method also has the effect of changing the weighting of companies in an index in precisely the wrong way and at precisely the wrong time from an investor's perspective. In particular, if a company buys back shares on the market, or insiders are buying large blocks of shares, indicating the belief that the company is undervalued, this operates to *reduce* the weighting of the company in the index. This is exactly the opposite of what an investor would want, i.e., investors would want an undervalued company to have a greater weighting in the index, not less. In other words, a company or an insider would typically only want to buy shares when prices are low relative to intrinsic value. However, such buying on the part of the company or insiders reduces the amount of publicly available shares, resulting in a reduction in weight in the index. Similarly, when a company issues shares in the market, or insiders are selling closely held shares to the public, indicating they believe the company to be overvalued in the market, this increases the company's publicly available shares, resulting in an increased weighting in the index. Since a company or an insider would typically only want to sell shares when prices are high relative to intrinsic value, the weight increase will also again likely be the exact opposite of what an investor would want.

Another ramification to the change to free-float based index weighting is the fact that, if a very large number of shares of a company are privately held, then that company may not have a sufficiently large float of publicly held shares to be part of an index at all. For example, if a company is 60% owned by its founder, who is an owner-operator, with the remaining 40% of the shares held by the public, only this 40% would now be considered as "free-float" shares for the purposes of its weighting in an index. This 40% of the shares may not constitute a sufficient number of shares, a sufficient amount of liquidity, for inclusion in an index. Hence, whereas prior to this change the company had a sufficient number of shares for inclusion in an index, with free-float based index weighting this would no longer be the case. Thus the free-float method of calculating index weighting has the effect of excluding some owner-operator companies entirely for consideration in an index. This is an unfortunate result, since such owner-operator companies are likely to perform better than other comparable agent-operator companies.

Hence, for variety of reasons, this change from a pure market capitalization weighted system to a free-float weighted system serves as a systemic constraint which is likely to reduce index fund performance over time. Even further, this change will create market price distortions in the stock prices of owner-operator companies. This is due to the fact that, as these companies are less heavily weighted in indices than heretofore they have been, the number of shares of owner-operator companies purchased when money flows into index funds will be less than it was before. Further, some owner-operators companies that would have normally been part of an index are now excluded from this possibility, due to their lack of a sufficient number of free-float (publicly held) shares. Thus shares of owner-operator companies will be less widely purchased due to indexation, and hence more likely available at bargain prices, than they otherwise would have been.

Therefore, indexation causes various market price distortions that are not readily apparent to the casual observer, but with the end result that market prices tend to deviate from correct prices.

5. Knowledge / Experience

The fifth requirement is that the people generally have at least a modicum of knowledge or experience that allows them to provide some type of informed estimate or opinion. Initially it would seem that this question can easily be answered in the affirmative. A tremendous amount of thought and intelligence is applied to the stock market, with most market participants having college degrees, many with business degrees or MBAs. In addition, many participants generate detailed quantitative analyses and computer-generated models to attempt to identify segments of the market for investment or to predict the overall movement of the market. Many others run stock screens based on price/ earnings (P/E), price/book (P/B) and other valuation metrics to attempt to identify bargain securities. Given the large amount of intellectual capability applied to earning money in the stock market, it appears virtually certain that a sufficient amount of knowledge and experience is being applied.

However, upon greater reflection, the question as to whether this requirement is met in a financial marketplace is somewhat more difficult to answer than it first appears. It can easily be argued that many, perhaps the majority, who participate in the stock market make their decisions on some combination of incomplete information or poor reasoning, or both. In particular, this requirement can be viewed as having two components with respect to formulating votes on stock prices: 1) a sufficient amount of intelligence is being applied; and 2) the intelligence is being applied using a correct analytical or decision-making framework capable of producing a correct result. With respect to component 1) above it is very clear that more than a sufficient amount of intelligence is being applied to the stock market as discussed briefly above. The real issue lies with component 2), i.e., do a sufficient number of people utilize a correct decision-making framework in formulating their votes on stock prices? For the purposes of our discussion here, the result of people's votes in the stock market, their buy and sell orders, ideally should be to drive current stock market prices toward correct stock prices, meaning the intrinsic values of the underlying businesses. Thus, when a person places a buy order to purchase a particular stock, in an ideal world this buy order would be predicated on the notion that the person has performed a somewhat intelligent appraisal of the value of the underlying business, and he is purchasing a piece of the business for less, hopefully much less, than his appraisal determines that it is worth. The above scenario occurs to varying degrees in some percentage of stock transactions. The unfortunate reality though is that many market participants conduct stock transactions without any real assessment of the underlying value of the business they are buying or selling.

In this author's admittedly opinionated view, different investment approaches provide different levels or degrees of closure between the current stock price and the correct stock price. The most efficient is a bottom-up value-based approach which, when done correctly, does the best job of driving current stock market prices toward correct prices. The bottom-up value-based investing approach involves estimating the intrinsic value of businesses based on a number of factors, and buying stock when the estimation of the intrinsic value is significantly greater than the current market price. A bottom-up value-based approach requires a considerable amount of knowledge, research and analysis, and is predicated on a sound analytical framework.

In contrast, a top-down approach begins with a survey of the macroeconomic climate, perhaps the global economy, and then attempts to determine which countries or market sectors are the best candidates for investment, usually based on macroeconomic predictions involving either potential growth or value. This approach then involves either a purchase of a broad array of stocks within this chosen sector or a further attempt to identify individual companies within this sector. Some type of fundamental analysis may be (purportedly) used in assessing sectors or companies within a sector for investment. A top down approach also requires considerable knowledge in its application, especially because an assessment of the macroeconomic climate is considerably difficult. In this author's opinion, the top-down approach is a less reliable decision-making framework than a bottom-up approach, primarily because correctly assessing the macroeconomic climate is much harder than correctly assessing a particular microeconomic situation, i.e., the value of an individual business. Thus the top-down approach may also do a fairly good job of driving stock market prices toward their correct prices, but not as efficiently as the bottom-up approach.

Technical analysis does not involve assessing the intrinsic values of businesses and comparing these values to current stock prices. Instead, technical analysis attempts to predict movements in the market based on how people have behaved in the past. In other words, technical analysis involves analyzing charts of previous stock price movements and attempting to predict future stock prices based on trends or patterns in the charts. Given that the goal of technical analysis is NOT to close the gap between price and value, but rather to profit from predicted movements in stock prices based on previous price movements, it is difficult to see what role technical analysis plays in the "wisdom of the crowd." Seemingly, the portion of the crowd that partakes in technical analysis is just as likely to drive the current stock price away from the correct price as towards it.

Some participants in financial markets simply do not use a correct analytical or decision-making framework in making their estimates of stock prices. For example, many participants utilize some form of modern portfolio theory in making stock market decisions, thus basing their decisions on an essentially incorrect decision-making framework. More specifically, modern portfolio theory makes certain assumptions which are simply not true, e.g., that people are rational actors, markets are efficient, risk can be quantified by various measures of volatility (e.g., beta), etc. No matter how great the intelligence that is being applied, if the decision-making framework is unsound, the resulting estimates will simply not be correct, or more generously will be less correct than they could have been. To take a simple analogy, assume an intelligent person is given a problem that requires a number of addition and subtraction steps in order to be solved. However, instead of using addition and subtraction the person generates complex covariance models to attempt to solve the problem, where unfortunately these covariance models do not produce the correct result. This analogy unfortunately describes a number of academically miseducated participants in a financial marketplace.

At the opposite end of the spectrum, many so-called investors buy stocks in companies for no apparent logical reason whatsoever, or using absolutely no analytical framework to arrive at their decisions. I know – I used to be one of them. Some buy stock merely because "it's a good company", or because there is some growth story put out by the press, without any consideration of the price they are paying for the underlying business, i.e., without considering the value they are getting for their money. Others buy stocks in "hot sectors", again without regard to price considerations. The truth of the matter is that value investing is hard mental work, and many people tend to shy away from such pursuits. In "The Art of Contrary Thinking", Humphrey Neill presented a section titled: "The Investor's Dilemma", where he discussed the propensity for market participants to make investments based on market forecasts, instead of bottom-up value based principles. Here Neill commented:

> Let us stress one psychological factor – a basic truism – that underlies the whole problem, because in the final analysis investment is a human problem.

> The average investor does not think and does not wish to think. Automatic forecasting methods relieve investors from sweating it out for themselves. They can "read" the findings of a given market-swing method and thereby avoid the backbreaking pick-and-shovel work that is necessary if one wishes to uncover the rich pay dirt that lies deeply buried. Prospecting for true values is hard work! [The] "buy values" concept is without question a sound approach, but it requires applied headwork and mental discipline. It will never be practiced by a large segment of the public.[27]

Neill's comments are as true today as when they were written in 1950. Valuing businesses is hard work, requiring some knowledge of accounting and financial statements, as well as an understanding of various businesses, including elements such as return on equity, capital allocation, quality of management, etc. Most people would rather buy a stock with much less thought involved, and hence that is what most people do, whether the stock purchase is based on a pundit's market prediction, a great growth story being discussed in the press, or some talking head's stock pick. The end result is that seemingly a small minority of investors applies the appropriate value-based analytical framework to stock selection.

Notably for the purpose of this book, Neill goes on to say:

> Thus, I dare to predict that contrary opinions will remain valid as a guide until public psychology changes – and it has not changed in centuries. So long as the investing public (any many of its advisers) acts as a "crowd," it'll pay to be contrary.[28]

Finally, we must consider the role of computer-based trading on stock prices. We have already discussed the short-term horizon of many market participants, measured in months or weeks, and sometimes days or even hours. Computer based trading is an even greater magnitude of short-termism, with many computer algorithms designed to eke out trading profits over the course of seconds or even microseconds. The effects of computer based trading are so short-term in nature that they are unlikely to register with most human participants. For the purpose of this analysis, it is presumed that, considered in its totality, computer based trading is likely neutral in its effect on stock prices, and at best operates to moderately drive current stock prices to their correct prices.

Considering all of the above, the question presented was: does a sufficient percentage of the "crowd" of market participants utilize an appropriate analytical framework and hence provide informed estimates on stock prices? Stated another way, taking all of the various inputs from the crowd, are these inputs sufficiently informed to allow the "wisdom of the crowd" to manifest itself in resulting stock prices? Certainly a portion of the crowd does a fairly good job in applying their knowledge and experience to drive current stock prices to correct stock prices. This is reflected in the fact that the overall market is largely efficient. For the participants who provide ill-informed votes on stock prices, it can be reasonably argued that their votes are likely spread both above and below the correct price, hence acting in the aggregate to move current stock prices toward their correct prices. On the other hand, it may well be that, when a current stock price is incorrect, e.g., above or below the correct price, these uninformed votes on stock prices may be evenly distributed above and below this incorrect price, and thus may not operate to bring any wisdom to the table in terms of correcting incorrect stock prices. This latter view may in fact be closer to reality than the former. However, even if this was true, and some segment of participants did not provide sufficiently informed estimates to drive current stock prices to correct stock prices, they apparently would not detract from this goal, but rather would seemingly neutralize each other. In this scenario, there are still a sufficient number of investors who do provide wisdom toward correct stock prices.

Overall, it is probably best to conclude that this criterion is largely met, i.e., that market participants on the whole have sufficient knowledge and/or experience to provide judgments on stock prices that, in the aggregate, constitute a form of wisdom. However, the fact that so many participants in the market do not use a correct analytical framework in their stock investments is certainly troubling.

6. Rationality

The sixth and last requirement is that the people making the decisions, the people voting on stock market prices, think in a rational manner in formulating their opinions. One of the principal assumptions in economic and finance theory in general is that people are "rational actors" or "rational wealth maximizers." As such, people should rationally and logically pursue the correct decision path to maximize their wealth. Therefore, classic academic economics and finance would say that this criterion is clearly met. This again brings to mind Yogi Berra's famous quote about theory and practice. The reality is that people generally are NOT uniformly rational when it comes to decisions about money and investments. This was recognized by Benjamin Graham in his 1934 edition of *Security Analysis,* and also in his 1949 book *The Intelligent Investor,* where Graham presents his famous "Mr. Market" metaphor for the behavior of the stock market, and how to opportunistically take advantage of the stock market. Graham writes:

> Imagine that in some private business you own a small share that cost you $1,000. One of your partners, named Mr. Market, is very obliging indeed. Every day he tells you what he thinks your interest is worth and furthermore offers either to buy you out or to sell you an additional interest on that basis. Sometimes his idea of value appears plausible and justified by business developments and prospects as you know them. Often, on the other hand, Mr. Market lets his enthusiasm or his fears run away with him, and the value he proposes seems to you a little short of silly.

> If you are a prudent investor or a sensible businessman, will you let Mr. Market's daily communication determine your view of the value of a $1,000 interest in the enterprise? Only in case you agree with him, or in case you want to trade with him. You may be happy to sell out to him when he quotes you a ridiculously high price, and equally happy to buy from him when his price is low. But the rest of the time you will be wiser to form your own ideas of the value of your holdings, based on full reports from the company about its operations and financial position.

> The true investor is in that very position when he owns a listed common stock. He can take advantage of the daily market price or leave it alone, as dictated by his own judgment and inclination. He must take cognizance of important price movements, for otherwise his

judgment will have nothing to work on. Conceivably they may give him a warning signal which he will do well to heed—this in plain English means that he is to sell his shares *because* the price has gone down, foreboding worse things to come. In our view such signals are misleading at least as often as they are helpful. Basically, price fluctuations have only one significant meaning for the true investor. They provide him with an opportunity to buy wisely when prices fall sharply and to sell wisely when they advance a great deal. At other times he will do better if he forgets about the stock market and pays attention to his dividend returns and to the operating results of his companies.

Thus Graham clearly realized the bipolar nature of the stock market, the manner in which the stock market can be beset by periods of fear and greed, swinging like a pendulum between unreasonably low prices during times of fear and depression and unreasonably high prices during times of greed and euphoria.

Another form of irrationality that is present during all stages of market cycles is the innate desire of people to "get rich quick" – the desire for instant profits. This tendency produces a short-term mindset in most participants, causing them to make decisions that for the most part are detrimental to their long-term financial performance. While the notion of short-term thinking was discussed above with respect to professional money managers in the section on decentralization, it deserves another mention here because this phenomenon is not limited to professionals who are being graded on their quarterly performance. Rather, short-term thinking is the predominant mindset among the vast majority of market participants, both professional and nonprofessional alike. A few byproducts of this form of irrationality are the unfortunate focus on "story stocks" which promise instant riches but tend to mostly result in disappointing losses, the tendency to trade too often based on expected near term catalysts, and finally, and perhaps most importantly, the tendency to ignore undervalued stocks which lack any obvious near term catalyst.

Academia has been slow to catch on to this reality of irrationality, but recently a new academic field referred to as "behavioral finance" has been developed to shed light on irrational behavior in markets. As a result, there are now a number of different types of psychological influences and biases that are recognized as affecting stock selection decisions. Discussion of each of these is beyond the scope of this book, but we will introduce a few of the most influential ones in Chapter 4. The result for our purposes is that many times the crowd as a whole generally does not think in a rational manner when voting on stock prices. To be fair, there is a relatively small group of investors (mostly in the value investing crowd) who for the most part behave rationally in formulating opinions on stock prices. Even further, many in this small segment are acutely aware of the irrationality of the broader market and purposely take advantage of the resulting mispriced stocks for financial gain.

The next question is the effect of the irrationality of the crowd on stock prices, i.e., does the irrationality of the crowd result in incorrect stock prices? Or does the irrationality of the crowd have little to no effect on stock prices, essentially canceling itself out. In other words, are people equally irrational both above and below the correct stock price, such that these irrational stock price votes cancel each other out? Here thought and experience would clearly indicate that irrationality has a markedly detrimental effect on the correctness of stock prices. The "get rich quick" mindset of most market participants tends to produce a conformity of irrationality on story stocks while also producing a general avoidance of companies that patiently and unglamorously compound their values at above average rates of return. Further, during times of extreme fear in the market (think 1929-1932, 1938, 1973-74, 2009, etc.) a large majority of the crowd reacts irrationally in the same direction, selling equities in a mad panic without regard to price. Similarly, during times of extreme greed (irrational exuberance) in the market (think

1922 – 1929, late 1960's, late 90's, etc.), the crowd reacts irrationally in the opposite direction, buying equities in a fervor without regard to price. One result of this irrationality is an extreme loss of diversity of opinion as noted above. When we consider other psychological influences on behavior (discussed later in Chapter 4), we see again that these psychological influences and biases tend to push people in a certain specific irrational direction. In other words, these influences and biases do not push people equally above and below the correct stock price. Rather, these influences and biases tend to push everyone either above the correct stock price or below the correct stock price. Thus irrationality skews resulting stock prices away from their correct prices.

Therefore, the sixth requirement that the crowd generally think in a rational manner in formulating their votes on stock market prices is clearly not met. The failure of this single criterion to be met is more than sufficient in and of itself for the wisdom of the crowd to fail to produce correct prices in financial markets.

Summary

Therefore, of the six criteria (requirements) necessary for the wisdom of the crowd to apply in a financial marketplace, most of these are simply not met. The only requirement that clearly does seem to apply is knowledge. It appears that market participants have sufficient knowledge and/or experience that allows them to provide somewhat informed estimates or opinions. However, the key takeaway of the above analysis is that five of the six criteria required for crowd wisdom are either nonexistent, lacking to a considerable degree, or lacking at least during certain periods of time. Independence very clearly does NOT apply to a financial marketplace at all. The degree of rationality required for crowd wisdom is also clearly lacking. Some forms of irrationality are always present in the market, while others are greatly accentuated during certain periods of the market cycle. Finally, while undeniably present during lengthy periods, diversity of opinion becomes largely absent when either fear or greed take hold. At or near the midpoint of the stock market pendulum there is certainly a sufficient diversity of opinion on the part of market participants to satisfy the diversity requirement. However, as the market pendulum approaches its extremes, and irrationality and herd behavior take hold, diversity of opinion seems to become more the exception than the rule. Decentralization is also lacking to some degree, as there are a sufficient number of systemic constraints in the market to skew stock prices away from their correct prices. Finally, for professional money managers the incentive to produce optimum stock market decisions is corrupted by countervailing incentives of maximizing personal income, job security, and the desire to avoid looking foolish. Thus five of the six requirements necessary for the wisdom of the crowd to be present in a financial marketplace are to varying degrees simply not met. From this we can conclude that a financial marketplace cannot possibly be routinely efficient, i.e., it cannot produce correct stock prices all of the time. In the remainder of this book we will examine the ramifications of this conclusion as well as how to generate better investment decisions based on this knowledge.

4. IRRATIONALITY IN A FINANCIAL MARKETPLACE

"The Wall Street analysts are brilliant people; they are better at math, but we know more about human nature."[29] – Warren Buffett

As we have seen, in attempting to apply the wisdom of the crowd to a financial marketplace, there are a number of requirements that are simply not met. Each of these criteria that we have determined to be lacking is itself a reason why crowd wisdom does not manifest in a financial marketplace. Thus there is not just a single reason why markets are not entirely efficient, but rather there are a host of reasons, ranging from a lack of independence among participants, a lack of diversity of opinion during times of extreme emotion, various systemic constraints, poor incentives, and an overall lack of rationality among participants. Henceforward we use the term "irrationality" to include any type of cognitive bias or psychological misjudgment, including a lack of independent thinking (or herd mentality) present among market participants. Thus we will use the term "irrationality" to encompass more than just the fifth criterion discussed above.

When considering the relative importance of irrationality vs. systemic constraints as causes of market price inefficiency, lack of rationality among market participants is likely the greatest cause of stock market folly. Given the widespread irrationality of people in financial markets, it is only fairly recently in history that academic observers began to identify this phenomenon. As noted above, Benjamin Graham clearly recognized the irrationality of the market in his 1934 book "Security Analysis" and also with his "Mr. Market" metaphor, quoted above, which appeared in "The Intelligent Investor" published in 1949. More recently, and somewhat late to the party, academia has begun to acknowledge this, creating the new academic discipline of "behavioral finance" mentioned above. Behavioral finance is still somewhat in its infancy as an academic discipline, but it is sufficiently developed to explain many of the psychological and cognitive errors that lead to inefficient markets.

Some forms of irrationality seem to be constantly present in the market, whereas others seem to ebb and flow with the tides of emotion. When emotions are running high in the market, whether it be fear or greed, these emotions seems to trump all other factors in producing mispricing. Here we discuss some of the primary psychological factors and cognitive biases that tend to affect human judgment and thus produce irrationality. A comprehensive discussion of the psychology of misjudgment as it applies to a financial marketplace, as well as recent advances in behavioral finance, is beyond the scope of this book. However, an introduction to the basic concepts of investor psychology is important to fully understand and appreciate the extent of irrationality present in financial markets. Such an understanding can assist the intelligent investor in both identifying and taking advantage of the resultant mispricings in the stock market.

A. Greed (Get Rich Quick Syndrome)

You see it in casinos, you see it in lotteries and you see it in the stock market. People generally have a tremendous desire to make money very quickly. Lotteries have succeeded in every society where they have been used, and they have always been lousy investments. The stock market equivalent of lottery tickets are growth stocks, where people hope to make large returns in a relatively short amount of time based on some type of growth story for a particular stock. In addition, many people buy stocks with the expectation of turning an even quicker profit, often in the nature of days or even hours. Thus most market participants are prone to reach for dramatic large returns, whatever the cost to them on an average or long-term basis. Given the short-term unpredictability of individual stock and overall market movements, these people are destined for a lifetime of disappointing returns.

We previously discussed the short-term trading mindset of professional money managers in Chapter 3 as a systemic constraint on professional market activity. We also noted that individuals (non-professionals) also seem to suffer from this short-term horizon mentality, despite the lack of any equivalent systemic constraint. Clearly, a "get rich quick" syndrome plagues most market participants. Over the last 50 years the average holding period on the New York Stock Exchange has diminished considerably, from about 7 - 8 years to less than seven months. With such a short holding period, there seems to be no way that the long-term earnings power of a corporation could be a factor in most investment decisions, i.e., long-term value creation as a factor in stock selection appears to be mostly irrelevant. In other words, if a person has an investment horizon of 7 months, he is apparently looking for positions (these simply don't fit the definition of investments) that must deliver value within that time frame, and stocks that do not provide the possibility of such imminent gains are of little use.

This myopic focus on short-term trading profits, at the expense of long-term wealth creation, creates a dislocation between stock market prices and "correct" prices, where correct prices are based on the estimated earnings power and performance of the underlying business over a lengthy period of time. Therefore, the true investor with a long-term investment horizon has a competitive advantage over speculators with much shorter trading horizons. As we discussed earlier, in the short run the stock market acts as a voting machine, with prices generally reflecting changing investor moods and sentiments more so than intrinsic value of the underlying business. However, in the long run the stock market acts as a weighing machine, where the underlying intrinsic values of businesses will eventually be reflected in stock prices. For an investor who buys bargain securities, a long-term investment horizon allows sufficient time for the earnings power and fundamentals of an enterprise to show through in the stock price, i.e., allows for the stock market "weighing machine" to register value.

Why do so many people pursue an investment strategy that is virtually certain to produce poor results over the long term? Certainly the innate desire we have to "get rich quick" is a large part of the answer. As Warren Buffett has commented: "People would rather be promised a (presumably) winning lottery ticket next week than an opportunity to get rich slowly." In addition, recent neurological research has provided somewhat startling insight to this question. This research indicates that the *anticipation* of making lots of money can actually feel better than the making of it.[30] In other words, the anticipation of making money is very exciting, whereas the actual receipt of the money may be less so, especially if this was the expectation all along. This is also true for any of various types of rewards – the anticipation of the reward is likely to actually feel better than the reward itself. Thus when a person with a "get rich quick" mentality buys a stock, he is generally fixated on the short-term movement of that stock. The anticipation of the stock price moving upward provides a small thrill, and is a form of entertainment, albeit an expensive one, much like gambling at the casino. Thus, even though a large number of a person's "quick money" schemes do not work out, the person has received substantial pleasure and entertainment value from the mere anticipation of making outsized returns. In this way, short-term trading in the stock market is really no different than gambling at the casino. Each is an expensive form of entertainment for those inclined to a "get rich quick" mentality.

Consider further the striking implications if people generally experience greater enjoyment from anticipating or thinking about a potential profit than actually receiving it. Since the anticipation of profit actually provides more enjoyment than its realization, many investment strategies actually emphasize short-term trading with lots of transactions, as this provides a much greater number of events where this anticipation can be experienced. In other words, a short-term trading strategy entails a large number of stock purchases, each with the hope and anticipation of gains. The sum total of "enjoyment" derived from this large number of anticipation experiences (even though they mostly have an unhappy ending) is greater than the sum total of "enjoyment" from a much smaller number of well considered transactions. Thus, such a short-term trading strategy may produce a much greater amount of overall enjoyment than a long-term strategy which involves buying only a few stocks over the course of a year. This is true even though a strategy of selectively buying very few stocks is more likely to produce better results than a strategy which involves the purchase of hundreds of stocks over the course of a year. Again, if the real enjoyment comes from anticipation rather than result, making a large number of stock purchases is going to produce greater overall enjoyment than just making a few, regardless of the end result. After all, if you consider stock purchases essentially as lottery tickets, why not buy a bunch of them, rather than just a few? Similarly, it is much more fun to make 1000 bets on your weekend at the casino than just one or two. Thus a person's psychological reward system actually provides greater incentive for him to take a large number of different short-term gambles, rather than make a few well-researched bets. Stated another way, the enjoyment gleaned from anticipating short-term profits from actively trading in the stock market, even though those profits rarely materialize, seems to be greater than the more boring process of selectively investing for long-term wealth creation. In summary, our brains are wired to receive greater enjoyment from short-term trading strategies than from long-term wealth generation strategies, even if the latter will almost assuredly provide better financial results over the long term.

Recent research also reveals that people place much greater emphasis on the size of the potential profit than on the probability of actually making it. People can easily and readily visualize making large sums of money, whereas performing the mental gymnastics of estimating the prospects for long-term growth of the underlying business is much more difficult. Thus, in the interest of minimizing mental effort, people tend to focus on the reward rather than the probability of the reward. People are also more responsive to changes in the amount of a reward at stake than to the changes in the actual probability of receiving it. Thus as the potential reward of a growth stock story increases, the attention paid to the likelihood of this growth stock story coming true decreases. Further, changes in the probability of a growth stock story coming true barely register with most people. The end result is that in most "get rich quick" stock schemes very little effort is put into determining the likelihood of the stock purchase actually paying off.

The innate desire for people to "get rich quick" is a form of irrationality that has a widespread effect on stock market participants. As discussed above, one of the symptoms of this irrationality is short-term trading, the active buying and selling of numerous stocks in an attempt to eke out short-term profits. However, as noted above, short-term trading strategies are mostly doomed to failure. As Warren Buffett has wryly noted, "The stock market is designed to transfer money from the Active to the Patient." In other words, these short-term strategies are apt to lose money in the long run, to the benefit of patient investors with long-term horizons. Another symptom of this irrationality is speculation in growth stocks without adequate consideration of the probability that these growth stocks will deliver the expected returns. So much attention is paid to the popular growth stocks, inflating their prices well above their intrinsic values, that numerous opportunities are created in the boring, less popular stocks, creating value opportunities for the patient, contrarian investor.

B. Loss Aversion

Loss aversion refers to the innate characteristic whereby people more strongly prefer avoiding losses over acquiring gains. Consider as an example a person walking down the street who finds a $100 bill on the ground and picks it up. Now consider the opposite scenario where a person reaches into his wallet and realizes he has lost $100. Based on psychological studies, the person losing the $100 would on average feel 2x – 3x as much regret as the happiness felt by the person who found the $100. As with many other biases, loss aversion most likely developed during prehistoric times, where the possibility of loss often meant the difference between survival and death. Thus sensitivity to loss was more beneficial to our survival than appreciation of gain, and correspondingly humans ultimately placed greater emphasis on "not losing" than on winning.

Loss aversion manifests itself in a number of ways in the stock market. For example, people are generally risk averse, and hence many people keep their investment money in "safe" fixed income investments or cash. History demonstrates that people are much likely to do better with equity investments over the long term, but the potential for a stock market crash, with the accompanying loss and regret they would feel, causes them to choose the perceived "safer" alternative. This occurs even in instances of extremely low interest rates where such investments are not likely to even keep up with inflation. Hence instead of offering "risk-free return" they offer "return-free risk" – virtually no return coupled with the almost certain risk that their money will lose purchasing power over the life of the investment. It should be noted that although people are generally risk averse, the amount of risk people are willing to take is itself cyclical and often varies based on the current circumstances. During prosperous economic times people feel more comfortable, and even though prices are driven higher by the speculating public, they unknowingly take on greater risk when they purchase assets at these high prices. Thus it can be said that people are generally risk averse at least until the sirens of a stock market boom or a sure-thing stock growth story appears. During difficult economic times people feel less secure and are more risk averse, and thus even though prices are driven lower by overall anxiety and fear, excessive (or misplaced) risk aversion prevents people from buying stocks at these very low prices. This cycle of risk aversion is one of the major causes of boom and bust cycles in the stock market, and is also one of the main reasons for underperformance, as people buy and sell at exactly the wrong times.

Loss aversion can actually manifest in several different ways, dependent on the conditions being experienced. During periods of slow and steady (and relatively undramatic) stock price declines, many partici-pants hold on to their losing positions for much too long, simply to avoid realizing a loss (and admitting error). In this instance there is usually no significant event that causes a precipitous stock price decline, but rather a slow deterioration in the fundamentals of the business causes a slow but steady decline in stock price. Loss aversion coupled with consistency bias and overconfidence bias (discussed below) causes participants to hold onto these losing stocks, despite mounting evidence that selling would be a wiser course. Selling a slowly deteriorating stock will lock in a loss, which due to loss aversion is quite painful. Instead, the hope is for an unlikely rebound in the stock price – anything to avoid a loss.

However, when the stock price declines become much more pro-nounced (and dramatic), and correspondingly the elements of fear and panic are introduced, a more extreme form of loss aversion ensues, caus-ing market participants to sell as quickly as possible to avoid even further dramatic losses. This typically occurs when a company is experiencing some type of troubling or threatening situation, which in actuality is usually some type of short-term solvable problem. During such times, people irrationally flee from the stock, selling without regard to value. This panic driven flight causes the price of the stock to often times get absurdly low. The sell-off is due to their aversion to loss, as well as to other psychological factors such as fear and herd mentality. When the possibility of extreme loss is present, people lose sight of both rationality and business fundamentals, and fail to realize that most any business, even one undergoing serious difficulty, can be a bargain at the right price. Thus, companies that are experiencing temporary problems are routinely oversold, resulting in bargain prices for the rational investor.

C. Problems with Uncertainty

In general, people have difficulty dealing with uncertainty, and do so badly. People tend to suppress uncertainty in a variety of ways, either by creating a false sense of certainty where none exists, or by falsely as-suming that the future will look pretty much like the present. Volatility is simply one form of uncertainty that people do not handle very well, and experience has shown that people are tempted to tamp it down and pretend that the world is a smooth place. Our brains are wired to detect patterns in information, regardless of whether a pattern actually exists in the data. Also, people form an image of the future based almost exclusively on current conditions and the recent past, and they fail to take into account the potential for change or cyclicality. Below we discuss some of the most important ways people deal with uncertainty, and how these can lead to errors in judgment in the realm of investing.

One way that people attempt to handle uncertainty is referred to as "recency bias." Recency bias refers to the tendency of people to think that trends and patterns observed in the recent past and present will continue unchanged into the future. In large part, this seems to be due to the fact that the vast majority of human development and experience has occurred during a much more primitive era, where the environment changed little from year to year. Thus for much of human history people could safely assume that the future would be pretty much like the past and the present. Thus our way of thinking is wired to believe that current conditions will persist. In other words, people tend to extrapolate past and present trends with unwarranted confidence, observing what has happened in the recent past, and what is happening now, and believing things will continue as they have into the foreseeable future. To use a simple example, most people after having eaten a large meal and being full simply cannot imagine being hungry. Likewise people that are hungry cannot imagine being full. Similarly, whatever the current economic climate, people seemingly cannot imagine any different state of affairs.

The stock market generally operates in cycles, forever swinging like a pendulum between times of extreme optimism and extreme pessimism. However, the concepts of credit markets and equity markets are a relatively recent phenomenon in human development, and people generally have a difficult time understanding and appreciating that in such markets cyclicality is the rule. Instead, if the stock market has been going up and the economy is doing fine, people tend to think it will always be so and will never change. Thus, during the height of the stock market boom in 1999, people were predicting above-normal growth to continue well into the future, and corporations were estimating similar above-normal growth in their pension assets. Likewise, when bad times occur, people think doom and gloom and cannot imagine better times. Although both our economy and the stock market clearly run in cycles, people tend to focus on only the current conditions and falsely believe that the future will be pretty much the same as the present.

To further illustrate this point, consider the analogy of driving a car. There is a reason a car is designed to have a very large windshield and a much smaller rearview mirror. This is because what is coming at you is much more important than what you are leaving behind. The driving conditions you will be experiencing in the immediate future are more important than the immediately preceding driving conditions. However, the way most people think about the future can be analogized to driving a car in a forward direction while looking solely in the rearview mirror as a guide to future road conditions. The immediate past may or may not be a reliable guide to what the future holds. At some point there will likely be a curve ahead in the road, and an accident is likely to ensue. Most people, with their obsessive reliance on the immediate past and present, will simply fail to appreciate the virtual certainty of changing conditions in the economic and market landscape.

Another way to consider the operation of cycles in the stock market is to think in terms of the very powerful concept of reversion to the mean. Trees don't grow to the sky, and very few things go to zero. As Herbert Stein famously said, "if something cannot go on forever, then it will stop." Reversion to the mean certainly applies to a financial marketplace. The twin concepts of cyclicality and reversion to the mean play out over and over in the stock market.

Howard Marks, in his excellent book *The Most Important Thing* spends several chapters on cycles and observes that "there's little as dangerous for investor health as insistence on extrapolating today's events into the future."[32] Marks also lays down the following two rules:

> Rule number one: most things will prove cyclical
> Rule number two: some of the greatest opportunities for gain and loss come when other people forget rule number one.

Other ways people suppress uncertainty are through consistency bias, confirmation bias and overconfidence bias. Consistency bias is the notion that people desire to be consistent with their past positions and decisions. In short, once people make a decision or take a position, e.g., by purchasing a security, they have an innate desire to remain consistent with that position. People resist changing their mind and admitting they were wrong. Confirmation bias causes people to seek out evidence that tends to confirm their currently held views, and suppress or ignore evidence that is counter to their views. Overconfidence bias causes people tend to have unwarranted confidence in their own abilities, making them less likely to question their decisions. The powerful force of social influence (herd mentality), discussed below, magnifies this overconfidence bias. Consistency bias, confirmation bias and overconfidence bias all work hand in hand with recency bias to greatly affect investor behavior and cause overreaction. Due to recency bias, people decide that the future will be pretty much as the present and that the future trend will continue. Having decided that the current trend will continue, people desire to remain consistent with this mindset, and will actively seek out information that confirms their belief, all the while remaining ever so confident in their ability to divine the future. All of these biases are techniques developed by the human brain to suppress undesirable uncertainty.

This powerful combination of biases, emotions and herd mentality causes the market to perpetually overshoot the mean in each direction, much like a pendulum. More specifically, the cyclicality in a financial marketplace is largely due to the above-discussed psychological biases in combination with the powerful emotions of fear and greed, all magnified by herd mentality. With this potent combination of psychological factors, and given the unchanging characteristic of human nature, the propensity of the crowd to overreact to conditions in financial markets and hence "overdo" both bull markets and bear markets is a virtual certainty.

The above biases also play a large role in the overvaluation and undervaluation of individual stocks, regardless of the position of the current market cycle. The combination of recency, consistency, confirmation, and overconfidence biases causes people treat the successful popular stocks as attractive for sure, and thus bid them up to high valuations. They treat unattractive stocks as if they are certain to fail, and price them below liquidation value. Hence the reason that value investors often take contrarian positions is that not only are they betting on the cyclicality of the overall market, they are betting on the reversion to the mean of individual stocks.

D. Affect

The "affect heuristic" refers to the simple fact that a person's decision-making process is affected by his current feelings and emotions. In other words, a person's strong likes, dislikes, and opinions, experienced as emotions such as happiness, sadness, excitement and fear, heavily influence the person's decisions. Thus the term "affect" here may be considered to be synonymous with "emotional response." Affect is a heuristic, or mental shortcut, that allows people to make decisions quickly and efficiently, although not necessarily accurately. The affect heuristic generally operates subconsciously to shorten the decision-making process, allowing people to make decisions without the inconvenient burden of having to think, i.e., without the burden of having to consider all of the various factors that would normally be necessary for an optimal decision. Thus when a person is initially presented with a situation or set of facts, the person's initial emotional response to the situation is a substantial factor in the person's ultimate conclusion or decision. Many people, knowingly or unknowingly, use their emotions as a crutch, as a substitute for thought. After all, it is much easier to act upon one's emotional response than it is to take the time and effort to carefully think through a problem.

For example, when the stock market is booming, the average market participant is affected by the easy money being made. His brain forms mouthwatering images of the potential gains. Thus, when confronted with decisions regarding how to allocate his capital, whether to make additional investments in high P/E ratio stocks, go on margin, etc., the emotional liking and happiness of making easy money tends to trump the more cautious and rational analytical side of his brain. Here the affect heuristic effectively produces a "willing suspension of disbelief" in the mind of the would-be investor, causing him to ignore the high valuations and other evidence of bubble behavior. Instead, due to the participant's extreme emotional attraction to easy money, he gets caught up in the euphoria. The end result is that his normal analytical thinking process takes a back seat to the emotional excitement of large easy gains.

In a dramatic stock market decline, the average market participant is emotionally affected by the mounting losses. His brain forms images of more money being lost, of poverty and despair, made all the worse by his inherent loss aversion. Thus when confronted with investment decisions, such as whether to sell the pieces of companies that he owns (his current stock holdings) at bargain prices, or whether to buy more of his current stocks or new businesses (new stocks) at these bargain prices, the emotional feelings of fear of further loss and outright despair trump the rational, analytical side of his brain that would tell him that prices are insanely cheap. In other words, the typical market participant's reaction to a market panic is fear and despair, i.e., generally unhappy feelings, and these unhappy emotions affect the decision-making process. Thus many participant's gut reaction to a market decline is to sell everything after a certain point, if only to put an end to the unhappy emotions.

E. Endowment Effect

The "endowment effect" refers to the propensity for people to ascribe more value to things merely because they own them. In other words, people ascribe more value to an item that they own than they would if they did not own it. This effect has been verified in a number of different research experiments, where people place different values on things before and after gaining possession of them. The endowment effect certainly applies to purchased securities, where people ascribe more value to a stock after they buy it. The endowment effect, consistency bias, confirmation bias, and overconfidence bias all act together and reinforce each other, which at least partially explains why people tend to hold on to losing stocks long after a point where they should have sold.

F. Anchoring

The concept of "anchoring" or "anchor points" was introduced in Chapter 1. As previously discussed, the concept of anchoring refers to the fact that the manner in which people estimate things is to begin with a given number or anchor point, which may or may not be relevant to the task at hand, and then adjust upward or downward from that anchor point. Numerous psychological studies have demonstrated that people generally do not sufficiently adjust from their starting anchor point. Thus in the stock market people are generally inclined to estimate the correct price of a stock by starting with the current stock price and adjusting from there. However, people generally will not sufficiently adjust from the current stock price, and hence their estimates will be off for at least this reason. Even more importantly, the current stock price may or may not bear any actual relation to the correct price, and merely adjusting from the current price in an up or down direction is very unlikely to result in a correct valuation. Finally, changing stock prices continually produce new anchor points for people's estimates, and this is yet another reason that people find it difficult to not follow the crowd.

G. Social Influence and Herd Mentality

The term "social influence" refers to the propensity for people to look to the thoughts and actions of others to guide their own behavior. Thus people tend to conform their decisions and behavior to match others, either because they believe that other people are more knowledgeable about the situation or merely because they wish to conform to the behavior of the crowd. Regardless, this phenomenon tends to cause large groups (the crowd) to act in a common way, which is often incorrect under the circumstances and grounded in insufficient information. Social influence may also be referred to as herd mentality, and this topic was discussed in some detail at the beginning of Chapter 3 in our discussion of "Independence." However, herd mentality deserves extra mention here because it is extremely powerful, especially in combination with other influences and biases. In fact, herd mentality can be considered as a type of "amplifying influence." Whatever the current biases or influences that are currently affecting members of the crowd, herd mentality is virtually guaranteed to magnify their effects. The intelligent investor must be on the lookout for events that are likely to cause various influences or biases to surface among members of the crowd. If such events are recognized, it is virtually certain that herd mentality will come into play.

H. Greed and Fear

There are no more powerful forces in the market than the emotions of greed and fear, or euphoria and depression. The concept of greed was introduced above in the discussion of "Get Rich Quick Syndrome." However, greed is a much more powerful and comprehensive emotion than merely the desire to "get rich quick." At its heart, greed is the basic desire to obtain wealth far beyond one's basic needs. The desire of people to "get rich quickly" is merely one aspect of greed, although itself a very powerful one. Greed causes people to lose sight of caution and risk, and hence pursue a course of action that is detrimental to their long-term performance. Similarly, fear is also a very powerful, paralyzing emotion, causing people to temporarily lose the ability of rational thought. Greed and fear thus cause people to lose sight of objectivity, risk awareness and overall rationality, and they also naturally give rise to herd mentality. As Warren Buffett has commented: "When people get fearful, they get fearful *en masse.*" In contrast, confidence comes back one person at a time. Also, "when [people] get greedy, they get greedy *en masse.*" Caution and risk awareness also seem to return one person at a time. Greed and fear, coupled with herd mentality, are largely responsible for the great pendulum-like swings in the stock market between greedy euphoria and fearful depression. This is unlikely to change.

I. Lollapalooza Effects

Financial markets present an almost ideal environment for the "Foolishness of the Crowd" to manifest itself. A financial marketplace is a large, very liquid, and very public marketplace of people making financial decisions, and all of the various emotions, psychological biases and influences come into play in some form or another. Much of the literature in behavioral finance has focused on the effects of individual influences and biases. However, considering individual biases and influences in isolation does not provide a complete picture, and may in fact be misleading. Thus, predicting behavior based on consideration of only one influence or bias would be a serious mistake. Rather, one should consider all of the attendant influences and biases in order estimate the overall influence coming to bear on behavior. The real power of these influences lies in their combination. Charlie Munger has popularized the term "Lollapalooza Effect" to refer to multiple biases, tendencies or mental models acting at the same time in the same direction to produce a much greater effect. Thus a "Lollapalooza Effect" refers to a condition whereby a number of psychological principles act in concert to produce a very high level of misjudgment or irrationality, much greater than any single psychological principle would produce on its own. When one observes a powerful and seemingly inexplicable irrationality at work, it is very likely that a number of influence factors are acting in concert to produce a Lollapalooza Effect, causing an extremity of irrational behavior that cannot be explained by any single influence alone.

Consider the example given above in the discussion of the Endowment Effect, where people tend to hold onto losing stocks longer than they should, i.e., where people are loathe to sell their losing stocks when an impartial analysis would clearly indicate this is the right thing to do. This phenomenon is not merely a result of the endowment effect, but rather is due to a host of influence factors operating together, including a combination of the endowment effect, anchoring, consistency bias, overconfidence bias, confirmation bias, and loss aversion. The endowment effect causes people to place a higher value on the losing stock merely because they already own it. People also anchor to the idea that a fair price for a stock must be more than they paid for it. Consistency bias causes people to want to remain consistent with their past actions – they made the decision to buy the stock so naturally they want to remain consistent with this action by holding on to it. In particular, they don't want to admit that they made a mistake, and selling the stock at a loss is a clear admission of a mistake. People are also overconfident in their decisions and tend to only seek out evidence confirming their prior decisions. Finally, loss aversion causes people to go to extreme lengths to avoid realizing a loss. Instead, people irrationally hold on to the losing stock hoping to recoup the loss. Philip Fisher wrote in *Common Stocks and Uncommon Profits* that, "More money has probably been lost by investors holding a stock they really did not want until they could 'at least come out even' than from any other single reason."[33]

Stock market bubbles and crashes are perhaps the greatest example of a Lollapalooza Effect in action. Stock market bubbles are at least a function of greed and its corollary, get rich quick syndrome, as well as affect heuristic, recency bias, consistency bias, confirmation bias, overconfidence bias, anchoring, and finally, herd mentality. Greed and get rich quick syndrome cause people to lose sight of objectivity in their mindless pursuit of quick riches. The affect heuristic causes people's emotions to trump rational decision-making. Recency bias causes people to view the recent run-up in stock prices and assume that the future will be more of the same. Due to consistency bias, people who have thought and acted as if stock prices will continue to rise feel the need to remain consistent with this view. They also seek out evidence confirming this belief while ignoring evidence to the contrary, and over-confidence in their abilities further prevents any self-examination of the correctness of their actions. The concept of anchoring causes people to estimate stock prices based on current prices. People naturally adjust their stock price anchor points upward in concert with increasing stock prices, making it difficult for them to accept lower, more realistic prices. Finally, herd mentality causes people to conform to the crowd, providing justification for their actions and reducing the chance that they will take an objective view of current affairs.

Similar to bubbles, stock market crashes are at least a function of fear and its corollary, loss aversion, as well as affect heuristic, recency bias, consistency bias, confirmation bias, anchoring, and finally, herd mentality. Fear and loss aversion cause people to lose objectivity and rationality in their desire to avoid loss. As described above, initially, due to loss aversion, people are reluctant to sell their losing positions despite the mounting evidence that their investment was a mistake. Eventually, as the losses continue to increase in magnitude, fear takes hold, and as a result loss aversion now manifests itself as the desire to get out of the position regardless of price. The affect heuristic also causes people to make rash, emotional decisions based on current fear-inducing circumstances. Recency bias causes people to view the recent decline in stock prices and assume that the future will be more of the same. Due to consistency bias, people who have thought and acted as if stock prices will continue to fall feel the need to remain consistent with this view. They also seek out evidence confirming this belief while ignoring evidence to the contrary, and their overconfidence in their abilities further prevents any self-examination of the correctness of their actions. Anchoring causes people to estimate correct stock prices based on current prices, and people naturally adjust their stock price anchor points downward in concert with decreasing stock prices, making it difficult for them to envision higher, more realistic prices. Finally, herd mentality causes people to conform to the crowd, providing justification for their actions and reducing the chance that they will take an objective view of current affairs. Fear and herd mentality are a particularly potent combination, as our brains are wired from prehistoric days to react to and emulate the fear and panic of others as a type of survival instinct. When a person observes a large number of others in a fearful or panicked state, it is extremely difficult for the person to maintain his objectivity and rationality.

Conclusion

Stocks are by and large the only asset class where the lower the prices get the less people want them, and the higher the price gets the more people want them. The cause of this unique and strange phenomenon is the presence of a large, very liquid market where humans make financial decisions, coupled with various forms of irrationality such as those discussed in this chapter. Some of the above biases are always present in the market to varying degrees, while others become very pronounced only under certain conditions. Whenever an event occurs which cause two or more biases or influences to take effect, the result is a much more powerful influencing effect that is likely to cause widespread irrationality on a large scale, and hence large mispricings of stocks. These events can either be of a macro or microeconomic nature. The goal of the intelligent investor is to be able to recognize these events, as well as the psychological influences and cognitive biases that will inevitably come to bear, and be poised to take advantage of them. This is the subject of the remainder of this book.

PART II. PROFITING FROM THE FOOLISHNESS OF THE CROWD - A PSYCHOLOGICAL FRAMEWORK FOR INVESTMENT

"Attractive opportunities come from observing human behavior. . . . Human behavior allows for success if you are able to detach yourself emotionally." – Warren Buffett[34]

"If you're going to buy the best bargains, you have to buy the things that people are selling." – Sir John Templeton

5. PREDICTABILITY OF THE FOOLISHNESS OF THE CROWD AS A BASIS FOR INVESTMENT

When a large number of people apply their judgment to a particular estimate, and certain criteria are met, the collective result represents a significant amount of wisdom, referred to as the "wisdom of the crowd." However, as detailed in Chapter 3, a number of these key criteria are not met in a financial marketplace, thus producing what we have called the "Foolishness of the Crowd." More specifically, as discussed above, there are various emotional, psychological and cognitive factors governing human behavior which inhibit rational thought in financial markets. These factors include a lack of independence of decision-making, producing a destructive herd mentality, as well as various emotions, cognitive biases and psychological influences that produce poor judgment. Also, the focus on short-term profits over long-term wealth accumulation, described above as a systemic constraint, can also be viewed as a form of irrationality. The "Foolishness of the Crowd" encompasses all of these tendencies toward irrationality in a financial marketplace, in all of its various forms. Note that irrationality is not the entire picture when it comes to explaining market inefficiency. Rather, various systemic constraints such as size constraints among large mutual funds, portfolio constraints, and the effects of indexation also contribute to market inefficiency, and these systemic constraints cannot be said to be caused by irrationality. The term "Foolishness of the Crowd" is used to refer to *all* of the various types of causative forms of market inefficiency resulting from a lack of crowd wisdom criteria, whether based on irrationality or systemic constraints. In other words, the "Foolishness of the Crowd" refers to the errors of the overall market in determining stock prices, including both the irrationality of the crowd as well as systemic constraints, each of which produces incorrect prices. The term "Foolishness" is used because it is the opposite of wisdom, and for the most part market inefficiencies only occur when crowd wisdom is not present, meaning that the "Foolishness of the Crowd" is present.

A large number of people participate in financial transactions every day in the stock market. Also consider that the previously discussed emotions, biases, errors in judgment and lack of independence affect virtually all of the participants to varying degrees. Given this widespread tendency toward irrationality, the Foolishness of the Crowd is likely to manifest itself in certain reliable and predictable ways, perhaps more so when certain factors are present and less so when certain factors are absent. Because of this, the following question presents itself: Is the Foolishness of the Crowd that manifests itself in the stock market sufficiently predictable and reliable to serve as a basis for investment decisions? In other words, can investment decisions be made at least partially on the basis that the Foolishness of the Crowd will reliably manifest itself in a predictable manner, at least under some circumstances. We believe the answer to this question is clearly yes.

Let's first consider the reliability of the Foolishness of the Crowd. Given the abject irrationality that is present to varying degrees in the stock market, the question arises as to whether this irrationality is sufficiently reliable to use as a basis for investment. For example, is irrationality simply a temporary condition of mankind, destined to disappear over time as we acquire greater intelligence and knowledge? We think not. We live in an ever-changing world--market opportunities change, industry sectors fall in and out of favor, the legislative and regulatory environment is constantly in flux, and globalization marches onward. However, perhaps the one constant in our ever-changing world is human nature. The way people think and behave, especially in markets, has not changed for at least 400 years since the first recorded market bubble (Tulipmania) in 1637, and it can be fairly safely predicted that it will not change in the next 400 years. Human beings have spent literally thousands and perhaps millions of years developing cognitive and psychological biases, many of which were adapted to facilitate survival in a more primitive environment. A similar length of time may be needed for these biases to become reduced in any recognizable way.

With respect to predictability, consider that financial markets present an almost ideal environment for the "Foolishness of the Crowd" to manifest itself. A financial marketplace is a large, very liquid, and very public marketplace of people making financial decisions (a recipe for crowd behavior), where the potential, or at least the aspiration, for making large amounts of money very quickly is ever present ("Get Rich Quick Syndrome"), where the possibility of financial loss is constantly present ("Loss Aversion", "Overconfidence Bias"), where people purchase things (stocks) with a disinclination to sell them ("Endowment Effect"), where the future of the market is uncertain and largely unpredictable ("Problems with Uncertainty"), where news of the recent past and present is widely disseminated ("Recency Bias", "Confirmation Bias"), and where everyone is acutely aware of the collective decisions of others ("Herd Mentality"). Let's examine each of these premises in turn with respect to the stock market.

The stock market is a large, very liquid marketplace with a number of people making financial decisions. This premise was addressed above in our discussion of the wisdom of the crowd. Clearly there are enough financial transactions performed each day in the stock market for some form of the wisdom of the crowd, or in our case the Foolishness of the Crowd, to be present. As noted above, between 50% to 70% of Americans participate in the stock market in some form, as well as a large number of international participants, and every day 1.5 to 2.5 billion shares trade hands on the New York Stock Exchange. Given the size of this crowd and the sheer number of transactions on a daily basis, some form of crowd result must be produced by this activity. As we will see, this crowd result is partly wisdom of the crowd and partly Foolishness of the Crowd.

A financial marketplace is also clearly a place where the potential to make a large amount of money in a short period of time is ever-present in people's minds. The instances in the literature where the stock market is compared with a casino are legion. The large number of daily stock transactions and the large amount of portfolio turnover suggest that patience is not a widely held trait among participants in financial markets. Recent medical research has also indicated that the area of the brain that "lights up" when a financial windfall occurs is the same area that lights up when a person uses mind altering drugs such as cocaine. People want to make money in the stock market and they want to make it quickly. Thus they are constantly shuffling in and out of positions, often at the wrong times and for the wrong reasons. Imagine that you sat down to watch the financial news at the end of the day, and the newscaster announced: "There was no trading today on the New York Stock Exchange. Everyone was happy with what they owned." On most days this would describe a value investor with a long-term orientation. To the vast majority of speculators, this would be laughable beyond belief.

The possibility of financial loss is also a constant fear among market participants. This fear is present on a security-specific basis and in the market as a whole. Every so often a market correction occurs, or a bubble bursts, causing a large drop in the market and widespread fear and panic among rank and file market speculators (individuals and professionals alike). Similarly, individual companies often go through times of financial distress, producing great fear and causing the speculating herd to run away en masse. Of course, these events also tend to produce a tremendous bargain opportunity to those few who can think rationally during these times.

That the future of financial markets is uncertain and largely unpredictable is beyond doubt. Near term predictions about the future course of the stock market are notoriously inaccurate. The stock market perpetually swings between unwarranted pessimism and unjustified optimism, but no one can reliably predict when these pendulum shifts will occur. The macroeconomic future is similarly unpredictable, prompting famed economist John Kenneth Galbraith to wryly note: "The only function of economic forecasting is to make astrology look respectable." In a slight twist on Galbraith's famous quote, Warren Buffett has commented:

> We've long felt that the only value of stock forecasters is to make fortune tellers look good. Even now, Charlie and I continue to believe that short-term market forecasts are poison and should be kept locked up in a safe place, away from children and also from grown-ups who behave in the market like children.

That financial news is widely disseminated, and hence everyone is acutely aware of the collective decisions of others, is also beyond dispute. This topic was discussed above in Chapter 3.

Irrationality among market participants easily produces large stock price distortions in the market, i.e., irrationality is easily the greatest factor in driving current stock prices away from correct prices. Irrationality affects the vast majority of all human participants in the stock market. Seemingly very few are immune to its effects. Due to the innate irrationality of human nature (our tendency toward emotional and psychological misjudgment), and also due to the particular characteristics of a financial marketplace, which seem ideally suited to draw out this irrationality in all of its myriad forms, the fact that the crowd or market will behave in a certain irrational (or foolish) way seems in large part predictably certain. In other words, just as the "wisdom of the crowd" will almost certainly present itself when certain factors are present, producing reliably good decisions, a primary thesis of this book is that the Foolishness of the Crowd will also reliably and predictably manifest itself, to varying degrees, when certain conditions are present. More specifically, when decisions or estimates are being formulated by a large number of people in a financial marketplace, and certain conditions are present, errors in judgment will reliably manifest in the result. Further, the manner, and to some extent the degree, in which incorrect stock prices are produced by the Foolishness of the Crowd is predictable, at least under some circumstances.

The Foolishness of the Crowd can be considered in the following manner. Suppose for a moment that all of the criteria discussed above in Chapter 2 were applicable to a financial marketplace, and the hence the wisdom of the crowd produced correct stock prices all of the time (Efficient Market Theory fantasyland). Now consider the same scenario, but where an offset is applied to the people's votes on stock prices. This "Foolish Offset" is due to irrationality or errors in judgment that are present to some degree in all of the participants and/or systemic issues present in the overall market (what we have collectively called the "Foolishness of the Crowd"). Irrationality will largely affect people in the same direction, although to varying degrees, with the average of this affect also contributing to the Foolish Offset being applied. Systemic inefficiencies will also certainly affect the overall market in a certain direction, contributing to this offset. It seems clear that this "Foolish Offset" will reliably be present to varying degrees under at least some circumstances. If the direction and amount of this offset can be estimated based on current market circumstances, or at the very least be anticipated to be present to a large degree under some circumstances, then intelligent investors can use their knowledge of the presence of this Foolish Offset, and their estimation of the amount of this offset, to help make informed investing decisions in the stock market.

Therefore, given 1) the large number of market participants; 2) the ideal conditions of large financial markets for irrationality on multiple levels; and 3) the proven and unchanging manner in which people act irrationally (or "less than wise") with respect to financial decisions; it is clear that a "Foolishness of the Crowd" result is present in a financial marketplace. In other words, financial markets produce a crowd result, but unfortunately in many instances this crowd result is not wisdom, but rather the result is offset from this wisdom by what we have termed a "Foolish Offset." Our contention is that, under at least some circumstances, this "Foolishness of the Crowd" result, this Foolish Offset from a normally wise result, is as certain and predictable as many other at-tributes in a financial marketplace. Further, under some circumstances this result is likely to be more certain and predictable than any macro-economic forecast or technical analysis, and in some cases may be as much a reliable indicator of stock mispricing as fundamental analysis would reveal.

Those who do understand the causes of "Foolishness", and can shield themselves from the tug of irrationality, are much more likely to keep their heads while everyone else is losing theirs. Further, those who are able to understand, perhaps even anticipate, the effects of "Foolishness" on stock prices are poised to take advantage of the resultant mispricings that occur. Knowledge of the "Foolishness of the Crowd" can thus be used as a guidepost for making sound investments in financial markets, i.e., as a reliable guide to the presence of bargains or values. Hence, the Psychology of Misjudgment as it applies to investment decisions, i.e., the "Foolishness of the Crowd", deserves to itself be an approach or style of investment. For perhaps the greatest affect, such Foolishness of the Crowd analysis should be applied alongside fundamental value invest-ing to help identify, assess and determine potential investments. This topic is discussed below.

The presence of widespread Foolishness or irrationality in a finan-cial marketplace leads to the conclusion that being contrary to this fool-ish crowd can often lead to exceptional financial performance. Here a brief discussion is warranted regarding the nature of contrary opinion, and why contrary opinion can be useful for financial gain. This top-ic was addressed by Edward C. Johnson II, the founder of the Fidelity Funds, in "Contrary Opinion in Stock Market Techniques", and his ob-servations are summarized below.[34] Recall the jelly bean example in Chapter 1. In this example, it is of little use to be contrary to the crowd, as there is likely significant wisdom from the crowd on this estimation. However, even more than this, it is very important to understand that the various opinions of the members of the crowd on the number of jelly beans in the jar has no effect on the correct answer – the actual number of jelly beans in the jar. In addition, consider various opinions on what the weather will be tomorrow. These various opinions will have no effect on what the weather will actually be tomorrow. The key here is that the opinions of the members of the crowd do not affect the fact under consideration. The actual number of jelly beans in the jar, and tomorrow's weather, are not changed by popular opinion. If there is a lack of independence, i.e., if the members of the crowd are aware of each other's estimates or predictions, then a herd mentality inevitably results, and the average of the estimates or predictions will most likely be skewed away from the correct answer. However, the actual fact under consideration remains unchanged.

Consider now a financial marketplace such as the stock market. Here the general opinion of the crowd has a profound effect on the prices in the market. For example, the general opinion as to whether the market should be going up or down has a clear effect on prices and the movement of the market. Similarly, the consensus view on whether an individual stock is over or undervalued has a direct effect on the price of the respective stock. As Howard Marks noted in *The Most Important Thing*: ". . . at the extremes, which are created by what 'most people' believe, most people are wrong." Marks also commented:

> What's clear to the broad consensus of investors is almost always wrong . . . . The very coalescing of popular opinion behind an investment tends to eliminate its profit potential.[35]

If the general consensus of the crowd is bullish, i.e., that stock prices are lower than they should be, the resulting votes from this consensus, the buy orders, will cause the overall market to rise. In addition, as everyone who believes that stock prices should be higher buys stock, this drives market prices to an extreme and necessarily creates a large pool of potential sellers. At some point in time this bullishness reaches an inflection point, whereby all of the potential buyers have purchased stock, and there are few if any more potential buyers to further increase stock prices. Once some previous buyers start to become sellers, or more generally once the number of those inclined to sell increases to out-number those inclined to buy, the market invariably declines. Thus the movement of the market in a certain direction often creates the impetus for its ultimate reversal. Again, as Howard Marks commented (and as quoted previously in Chapter 2):

> But whenever the pendulum is near either extreme, it is inevitable that it will move back toward the midpoint sooner or later. *In fact, it is the movement toward an extreme itself that supplies the energy for the swing back.* (emphasis added)
> FIRST QUARTER PERFORMANCE," APRIL 11, 1991"[36]

Another way to think about this is the importance of an investor dis-tinguishing between: 1) the attractiveness or favorable future prospects of a particular business; and 2) the attractiveness or favorable future prospects of a particular investment. These two concepts very often do not go together, the key difference here being the all-important factor of price. In the former, a business may have very favorable near term or long-term prospects, but the selling price being asked for a piece of the business may be so high as to make it an unattractive investment. In fact, the greater the consensus regarding the attractiveness of the company, the less likely the company is an attractive investment.

Consider the following gambling analogy. First assume a horse race with only two horses and 100 bettors each buying a $1 betting ticket, so that the total pot is $100. If 50 bettors bet on horse A and 50 bet on horse B, the 50 winners will pocket the entire $100, or $2 per person. Hence each winner will have doubled his $1 "investment." Now assume that horse A is a heavy favorite to win, and hence the vast majority (say

95 out of 100) of bettors bet on horse A to win. If all goes according to plan, these 95 bettors will share the total $100 pot, each receiving a little over $1 per person. Hence these bettors will have won virtually no money. In fact, by being right with the overwhelming majority, these successful bettors will most likely have lost money due to the various frictional costs of betting, e.g., house expenses, outstripping their betting gains.

This same reasoning holds true in financial markets. When a majority of market participants agree on the attractiveness of a company and buy its stock, the price of the stock rises. This rising stock price reduces the potential for any investment gains from the company that would result from its continued operational success. In other words, the strongly positive consensus on the attractiveness of the company operates to reduce the potential for any investment gains owing to the company's success, i.e., at least some amount of the company's operational success is already "priced in" to the stock. The rising stock price also increases the magnitude of potential loss if the company's operational performance disappoints in any material way. Many market participants often erroneously interpret a stock rise as confirmation of the underlying company's attractiveness. In truth, a rising stock price really just means that the market is reducing a person's odds of making money on the investment and increasing the odds of him losing money.

In a similar manner, when a majority of market participants agree on the current unattractiveness of a company and sell its stock, the price of the stock falls. This falling stock price increases the potential for investment gains from the company that would result from its operational success, whether turnaround or otherwise. In other words, at least some amount of the company's poor performance is already "priced in" to the stock, and the strongly negative consensus on the company operates to increase the potential for investment gains if the company exceeds its expected poor performance. The falling stock price also reduces the magnitude of potential loss if the company's operational performance continues to disappoint. Many market participants often erroneously interpret a fall in the stock price as confirmation of the underlying company's lack of attractiveness. In truth, assuming the problems facing the company are temporary in nature, and the underlying business franchise is sound or capably of recovery, a falling stock price really just means that the market is reducing a person's odds of losing money on the investment and increasing the odds of him making money.

Therefore, to a large degree, the profit potential of contrarianism in stock market investing can be viewed as resting on the following fundamental notions of the market:

1) People's views and opinions on stock prices decidedly affect the prices themselves;

2) The market will exhibit inefficiencies in the short term – there are psychological and systemic forces at work in the stock market that cause the crowd to reliably overshoot the correct price for a stock in both directions, often in a pendulum like manner. Stated another way, the Foolishness of the Crowd is oftentimes at work in the stock market, causing a Foolish Offset to be applied to the wisdom of the crowd result, i.e., a Foolish Offset applied to the correct price; and

3) Market inefficiencies typically do not exist for very long, and a company's stock price will eventually return (or at least cross over) to its correct price (the company's intrinsic value). Another way of saying this is that the Foolish Offset for particular securities will eventually disappear over time, with the resultant stock price reflecting only the crowd wisdom.

Investors can best profit from these market inefficiencies using one or both of the following two approaches:

1) The investor who is able to accurately estimate the intrinsic values of businesses is in a position to detect and take advantage of these market inefficiencies. Where the investor's estimation of intrinsic value of a company differs from the company's quoted market price in a sizeable

way (thus providing a large margin of safety), then the investor has identified a market inefficiency, and the company is suitable for investment;
and/or

2) The investor who is able to accurately assess when, and to what
extent, the conditions for market inefficiency are present, i.e., is able to
assess when one or more of the criteria necessary for crowd wisdom to
manifest are lacking, and hence the Foolishness of the Crowd is present,
is also in a position to detect and take advantage of these market inefficiencies. Where the investor detects clear Foolishness of the Crowd conditions or behavior, there is a good likelihood that a company's quoted
market price will be offset (by a Foolish Offset) from the normally wise
result, resulting in a mispricing and hence making the company suitable
for investment.

The first approach above is the classic value investing approach and
of course is highly recommended as the paramount method of investment. The problem here is that calculating (or estimating) intrinsic
values of businesses is difficult, time-consuming work, and can sometimes be fraught with error. In at least some instances even the best
value investor will have incomplete information, will misinterpret the
available information, or will fail to correctly predict the future course
of the company, and his intrinsic value estimate will be so incorrect as
to lead to poor results. The second approach is the focal point of this
book. The problem with this second approach is that properly assessing
Foolishness of the Crowd behavior or conditions can also be fraught
with error. Sometimes the crowd is fearful with respect to a particular
company for good reason. Other times, the crowd wisdom criteria that
are observed to be lacking are not in and of themselves sufficient to
provide the necessary conviction with respect to a proposed investment
opportunity.

While in this author's opinion either of these two approaches can
be practiced in isolation and lead to good overall results, by far the best
investment results come from combining them. Thus, in addition to the

classical value investing mantra of intrinsic value and margin of safety, a fundamental premise of this book is that the intelligent investor who is also acutely aware of the psychological and systemic forces at work in the stock market, and actively tries to identify and take advantage of these phenomena, is in a much better position to both detect and take advantage of these market inefficiencies. This is the primary subject of the remainder of this book.

6. IDENTIFYING MARKET INEFFICIENCIES

Now that we understand the inherent "Foolishness of the Crowd" in a financial marketplace, the next step is to understand how to take advantage of this knowledge to improve investment performance. Here we discuss some of the ways the intelligent investor can benefit from this knowledge, as well as some specific actions the investor can take to increase his resolve and confidence during periods of market folly. In chapter 7 we will propose an investment framework based partially on an understanding of the Foolishness of the Crowd, i.e., crowd irrationality and resulting market inefficiency.

Using the Foolishness of the Crowd to Identify Bargains

The stock market as a marketplace can be overwhelming in terms of the sheer number of choices available. Well over 5,000 companies are listed on the New York Stock Exchange and the Nasdaq, and an even greater number of mutual funds exist in the United States. Combine this with the large number of stocks and mutual funds on the European, Canadian, Japanese, and Hong Kong exchanges, as well as the various emerging markets, and the number of potential investment opportunities is staggering. Globally there are over 50,000 publicly traded businesses. Further complicating this search is the fact that, for all of our discussion of market inefficiency and the Foolishness of the Crowd, the stock market is largely efficient. The degree of efficiency of the market depends in large part on where it stands in the current cycle or movement of the pendulum. As discussed previously, the course of the stock market can be viewed as a pendulum that is forever moving between periods of fear and greed, despair and euphoria. The market is more

efficient near the midpoint of the pendulum swing and becomes less efficient as it moves toward the extremes. Regardless, at any point in time,
it can generally be expected that a large number of companies will be
fairly priced.

Thus the question arises as to how the investor can wade through
the large number of fairly priced companies to identify the potential
bargains. In truth, a large part of investing is simply being able to identify potential stocks or sectors in the stock market for further in-depth
analysis. Given the large number of choices available, how is the investor to identify a handful of companies for potential investment? What
methodology can he use to find the proverbial needles in the haystack?

An investor needs some shortcuts or heuristic methods to identify potential bargain opportunities in this large universe. One of the
most conventional shortcuts that investors use is a computer-based stock
screen that utilizes metrics such as low price/earnings, low price/book,
low EV/EBITDA, low price/sales, and other potential indications of value. While these screens can be useful, they often turn up a number of
companies that are priced low according to these metrics for a reason.
After the stock screen is run, a considerable amount of work remains
to sort through the results to find potential bargains. Even so, stock
screens and other similar tools can be very useful in identifying companies for further research and investigation.

A second shortcut technique, one perhaps most famously promul-
gated by investor Mohnish Pabrai, is the concept of "cloning", or copying
selected investments of other great value investors. The cloning strategy
involves following the recent investments of other notable value investors, and using this much smaller universe of investment ideas as the
basis for further analysis. One way to implement this cloning technique
is by studying SEC 13-F filings of respected value-based hedge funds or
holding companies. Form 13F is a quarterly report of equity holdings
filed by institutional investment managers with at least $100 million in
equity assets under management. An investor can review these SEC filings to determine both new and existing stock positions held by these

various hedge funds. Several websites track these 13-F filings and provide information on hedge fund stock positions, such as whalewisdom.com and dataroma.com. Other websites are available which provide value investment ideas and commentary, such as gurufocus.com, SumZero.com and the Manual of Ideas. Another type of cloning technique involves participating in any of the various value investing Internet forums to benefit from the wisdom of other value investors. These forums include Value Investors Club, Corner of Berkshire & Fairfax and other similar forums. These cloning techniques are essentially based on the wisdom of the crowd, in this case utilizing a small, select crowd of successful value investors as a truly wise crowd. Cloning is a very useful investment technique and is highly recommended.

A third shortcut technique that is espoused here is for the investor to use his understanding of how and why crowd wisdom sometimes does not apply to the stock market to successfully guide his search for investment opportunities. Bargain securities can only really exist where the market is not efficiently pricing the security, and as we have seen market inefficiencies for the most part only exist where one or more of the criteria for market wisdom are lacking. This lacking criteria can be any of the forms of irrationality or systemic inefficiencies discussed above, what we have called the "Foolishness of the Crowd." One of the most important benefits of our knowledge of the Foolishness of the Crowd is to understand exactly why the market is not efficient. This knowledge of *why* the market is not efficient will directly lead us to an understanding of *where* to look for these inefficiencies. Of the various shortcut techniques for identifying potential bargains in the stock market, the "Foolishness of the Crowd" technique is perhaps the most useful of all. In addition, this technique can be combined with cloning techniques discussed above, as well as stock screens, to produce a very powerful combination for identification of desirable investments.

A report titled *Alpha and the Paradox of Skill* by Michael Mauboussin of Credit Suisse discussed an interesting aspect of the life of Jim Rutt, the CEO of Network Solutions. As a young man, Rutt had the desire to become a better poker player, and to that end he spent a great deal of time learning the odds of each hand and how to detect "tells" in other players that gave away their position.

>At that point, an uncle pulled him aside and doled out some advice. "Jim, I wouldn't spend my time getting better," he advised, *"I'd spend my time finding weak games."*

>Success in investing has two aspects. The first is skill, which requires you to be technically proficient. Technical skills include the ability to find mispriced securities (based on capabilities in modeling, financial statement analysis, competitive strategy analysis, and valuation all while sidestepping behavioral biases) and a good framework for portfolio construction. *The second aspect is the game in which you choose to compete.* (emphasis added)

The uncle's advice was that the easiest way to win at poker is to spend time identifying easy games in which the other players are less competent and make mistakes, and then only playing in those games.

As another example, consider a hypothetical college football team that is operating from a clean slate for its upcoming season, with no games yet scheduled and no practices under its belt. Assume also that the sole metric for the team is its post-season win/loss record. In other words, assume that there is no credit given for strength of schedule. Rather, the team's win/loss record is the only thing that matters. Note that this is somewhat similar to actual college football, where teams routinely schedule easy non-conference opponents for guaranteed wins. Assuming this hypothetical situation, what should the coach / athletic director do to ensure the best possible results – the best possible win/ loss record? Of course the coach will work to improve the skill of his players through practices, weightlifting, watching opponent's game film, etc. By improving his team's overall ability, the coach increases his team's chances of winning games. However, there is a second, more effective strategy to increase the team's chances of winning its games – a way that is more likely to produce good results than merely increasing the team's skill level. This second strategy is to uniformly schedule weak opponents. Certainly if the coach is able to fill his 11 game schedule with much inferior opponents, such as small junior college teams, his chances of a winning season go up dramatically.

Thus if a player or team can routinely play against greatly inferior opponents, where the player/team has a huge skill advantage relative to the opponents, the chances of victory are obviously much higher. In most any competition or game, the absolute skill of the player (or team) is important, but it is not necessarily determinative of the player's success. What really matters is the *relative* skill of the players – how much better a player is relative to his opponents.

The investment process is very similar to these sports analogies. All that an investor really cares about is the total money he has at the end of his investing period. The difficulty of a person's investments does not change the final score. In other words, after the investing period is over and the investor has turned in his investment scorecard, the investor's "strength of schedule" – how difficult his investments were to analyze – does not factor in to adjust his end results. The investor who lagged the S&P benchmark by a wide margin is not likely to raise in his defense how he chose to pursue difficult, hard to understand companies as investments. Whereas a football team that schedules a very tough opponent may be somewhat satisfied (although they would never openly admit it) with a respectable loss, the investor is unlikely to brag about or even gain solace from how difficult his losing investments were. Certainly there are no "style points" given for tackling the hard investments. As Warren Buffet has said, "I don't try to jump over 7-foot hurdles: I look for 1-foot hurdles that I can step over."

The investor thus essentially has two ways to improve his investing results. The first way is for him to become more proficient as an investor, improving his skills in reading financial statements, his knowledge of businesses, and overall becoming better at valuing companies. The second way is to actively search for areas of the market where he has weak competition, e.g., where he has some type of edge over other participants. Many investors focus exclusively on the first path, honing their value investing skills. While this is undeniably important, we would argue that the second path is at least equally important. Perhaps the easiest and most important thing that an investor can do to improve his results is to intelligently select areas in the market where inefficiencies, the deviation of stock prices from their underlying intrinsic values, are likely to occur – where market participants will likely have made mistakes in valuation. The investor can then focus his valuation skills on this much smaller, focused universe of potential investments. This universe will by definition contain a much higher percentage of mispriced securities, greatly improving the investor's chance of selecting good investments.

Thus the investor's time is wisely spent identifying, and only participating in, areas of the investment world where market inefficiencies are likely to occur, essentially where other participants are making mistakes. As we have discussed, market inefficiencies are most likely to occur in situations where the wisdom of the crowd does not apply. Each of the reasons presented in Chapters 3 and 4 serves to create a distortion in stock market prices – a displacement between the price the market places on a particular stock and what the correct stock price should be. Hence each of these reasons is an avenue or a roadmap that identifies a particular company, or segment, of the stock market that is likely mispriced. A more detailed discussion of how to identify bargains based on particular aspects of Foolishness is presented below.

There are some forms of market inefficiency that seem to perpetually exist in the stock market. These market inefficiencies are due to various systemic constraints, primarily due to the short-term mindset of the vast majority of market participants, size constraints on large mutual funds, mutual fund portfolio constraints and the rise of indexation. These ever-present forms of market inefficiency can be analogized to some portions of the haystack that are perpetually glowing to indicate where the needles are located. We will discuss each of these in turn.

The short-term mindset exhibited by most would-be investors is perhaps the greatest advantage to the true investor. The market inefficiencies produced by this short-term mindset are many and varied. In many instances this short-term mindset causes the market to value a company based solely on what its anticipated results will be in the next quarter. Thus, for those companies that have latent earnings power – earnings power that appears to be clearly present to the investor, but which will likely not manifest in reported earnings until several quarters into the future, the market will in many cases not factor these latent earnings into the stock price. Rather, the market's focus on next quarter's earnings will tend to underprice the value of such a company relative to its true intrinsic value. The true investor who takes a long-term view, who is more interested in the slow and steady compounding of wealth than the desire to "get rich quick", can actively search for instances where a company has earning power that is not being priced into its valuation because it will not appear within the next few quarter's earnings. The investor can purchase such companies with the expectation that, when this latent earnings power is finally reflected in reported earnings, the market will reappraise the valuation of the company to reflect the company's true earnings power.

Size constraints and indexation both tend to favor the inclusion of larger, more liquid companies into mutual funds and index funds, respectively. The more money that is flowing into these mutual funds and index funds, the more that the stock prices of these larger, liquid companies gets driven up, regardless of underlying values. This inflow of money into these funds tends to have the opposite effect on smaller and/or less liquid companies, as less cash in the overall market is available to be allocated to these companies. As a result, companies which are smaller and/or insufficiently liquid will often be underpriced in the market relative to the larger, more liquid companies. Thus one criterion to consider in the search for investments is to consider whether the respective company is present in any of the popular indexes. One strategy would be to simply concentrate on companies that are smaller in size or which are not present in the indexes. For example, companies run by owner operators with larger insider ownership will often be somewhat underpriced in the market, simply because the large insider ownership results in less overall market liquidity of the stock, thus either reducing the company's exposure in the indexes or preventing it from being included altogether.

Other forms of market inefficiency seem to rise and fall with the emotions of the market. During times of extreme emotion, i.e., times of extreme fear and greed in the marketplace, virtually the entire haystack is glowing, and there are seemingly more needles than hay in the haystack. Our knowledge of the causative factors producing the Foolishness of the Crowd can be used to identify these needles – these bargains in the stock market. Let's examine more fully these causative factors that seem to present themselves under certain conditions, and how they can be used to identify stock mispricings, both underpriced bargains as well as overpriced stocks to be avoided. What we will quickly discover is that usually it is not just a single factor, a single aspect of irrationality or foolishness, that is producing a mispricing in the stock market. Rather, in most instances a number of different aspects of irrationality combine together to create a Lollapalooza affect, a magnified irrationality effect caused by a number of self-reinforcing aspects of foolishness acting in concert. In fact, except for the powerful emotions of fear and greed, one can argue that only one form of irrationality, acting alone, is generally insufficient to create a mispricing in the market. Rather, a combination of multiple forms of irrationality is usually required to produce incorrect market prices. Thus instead of discussing each form of irrationality and its effect on market prices by itself, we will discuss the scenarios where incorrect market prices are common are most likely to occur. Here we will discuss two principal scenarios: 1) when a particular company is "in favor" and performing well in the recent past, and hence is likely overpriced; and 2) when a particular company is "out of favor" or facing some type of short-term difficulty, and hence is likely underpriced. In performing this analysis, it is helpful to examine each of the causative factors of the Foolishness of the Crowd in a checklist manner, and then consider how these causative factors interrelate, complement each other and magnify each other to produce the necessary Lollapalooza effects for market mispricing to occur.

The "In Favor" Company

A company that is currently "in favor" is one which is currently performing well and also has been performing well in the recent past. For a company that is currently "in favor", the recent trend will be quite favorable, likely with a recent increase in stock price, and quite possibly a corresponding increase in reported earnings as well. Let's now examine the possible forms of irrationality that may affect the stock price of such an "in favor" company.

We will first consider the role of uncertainty, and in particular the manner in which people handle uncertainty. As discussed previously, most people simplistically assume that whatever the current trend is, that the trend will continue far out into the future. People tend to predict the future solely by gazing into the rearview mirror at the immediate past. Hence when conditions are favorable for a business, even a business known to be cyclical, and the stock price has been steadily moving upward, people will incorrectly presume that the current positive trend will continue. Thus they are likely to bid up the stock price to reflect future growth well into the future that is mostly predicated on a linear extrapolation of the recent past.

If the company is a "story company", i.e., has a sort of sexy growth story behind it that people can latch onto, this can add significantly to the excess incorporated into the stock price. As examples of this, consider the many Internet companies launched in the late 1990's, many of which had little revenue, no profits, but a great story: "The Internet will change the world!." As it turned out, the Internet did change the world, but not to a degree that would enable a company with a very poor business model to succeed as an investment when purchased at an excessively high price. As these words were written, Tesla Motors is the current "story company", and currently trades at over 100x next year's earnings forecasts. Here the story behind Tesla is how the electric car company changes the world. Perhaps it will, but so much growth is currently factored into the share price that very likely many investors will be disappointed. The reason why a "story company" can become more overvalued than the typical "in favor" company is the manner in which the "story" behind the stock affects people's views of uncertainty. We know from our prior discussion that people have a strong tendency to suppress uncertainty, principally be extrapolating the recent trend far out into the future. The exciting story behind the growth stock causes an even greater suppression of uncertainty, an even greater suspension of disbelief. This tends to cause market participants to bid up the stock price with even greater confidence. Further, as more and more members of the crowd believe in this story, the requirement of diversity of opinion that is so necessary for the wisdom of the crowd is lost. The moral of this "story" is that when a company has an emotional or exciting growth story behind it, the value investor should tread with extreme caution.

Short-term thinking and get rich quick mentality are also very important factors here. Due to people's natural tendency toward short-term thinking and the desire to make lots of money quickly, they will myopically focus on the short-term predictions of the company's performance. A company's stock price ideally reflects the discounted value of all future cash flows. The unfortunate thing that most people forget is that for an "in favor" company the favorable estimate of next quarter's earnings is very unlikely to be repeated for a great length of time, and certainly cannot go on forever. Since most people believe that the great results they have recently experienced and expect next quarter will continue out well into the future, or perhaps they don't think about anything beyond the next quarter, they tend to overweight future expected growth into the stock price. The fact that so many members of the crowd are affected by the psychological influences of mishandling uncertainty, short-term thinking and the desire to get rich quick, the stock price will be influenced by these factors and will very likely be pushed above the correct price.

This is a time when great care is needed to prevent investment loss, and the investor should be extremely cautious. A good rule of thumb is that the investor should proceed with extreme caution when investing in either: 1) a young company that promises to deliver fantastic growth in the future, or 2) a company that is currently "running on all cylinders", i.e., has been performing well in the recent past. Of course, there are exceptions to this rule, and there are some companies that have been able to compound value at a high rate for a lengthy period of time, notable examples being Berkshire Hathaway, Markel, Leucadia, Coca Cola, Walmart, etc. However, for every example of a great growth company, there are dozens if not hundreds of "high flyer" companies, i.e., companies whose stock price rose based on unreasonable expectations of future growth, only to have the stock price fall dramatically when the expected growth did not materialize. There are also many examples of companies that benefitted from a favorable tailwind for a short period of time, and whose stock price was driven well above intrinsic value based on the hope and expectation that currently favorable results would continue well off into the future.

How can our knowledge of the Foolishness of the Crowd help us? What the Foolishness of the Crowd tells us is that companies that are merely experiencing a short-term growth spurt will very often be priced as if they are long-term compounding machines. In other words, due to the psychological factors at play, a company that is currently but only temporarily "in favor", i.e., has been experiencing favorable results in the recent past but will not be able to maintain its current growth rate for anything approaching a lengthy period of time, will very often have a stock price that does reflect a scenario of long-term growth. In many instances, even if some semblance of the anticipated growth does materialize, the investor has likely already overpaid for this growth in his purchase price of the stock.

In attempting to assess whether a company is poised for long-term compounding of value vs. merely experiencing short-term growth, there is no substitute for a thoughtful, analytical study of the qualitative and quantitative aspects of the underlying business. This analysis will necessarily include an assessment of the long-term prospects of the business, including both the staying power of the business as well as its growth runway, the quality of the management in terms of capital allocation and shareholder orientation, and a host of other factors which are beyond the scope of this book. Suffice it to say that identifying the truly great future growth companies is extremely difficult, and much more often than not hopeful investors end up overpaying for growth that never materializes. Perhaps the best strategy is to attempt to identify a list of companies that are potential compounders, i.e., that have the potential to grow intrinsic value or book value for the foreseeable future, and patiently wait for one or more of these companies to encounter some type of short-term problem or issue. When this occurs, there will very likely be an overreaction in the ensuing stock price decline, and hence providing a good entry price for the investor. This is the subject of our next section.

The "Out of Favor" Company

When conditions are temporarily unfavorable for a business, for example the business suffers some type of short-term setback or difficulty, people tend to overreact negatively to this uncertainty, and they also presume that these dark times will last forever. Here again, due to the manner in which people mishandle uncertainty, most will blindly assume that the current situation will continue far out into the future. Thus people are likely to bid down the stock price to reflect the presumption that this negativity will continue well into the future. In addition, during times of negative uncertainty, people have a strong tendency to factor in a greater amount of negativity into the stock price than is warranted. In other words, people tend to overreact to bad news. Thus the stock price will reflect this extreme negativity. However, reversion to the mean, the tendency for things to revert to their average state or performance, is a very powerful force. Presuming the investor is convinced that the business itself remains viable as a going concern, it is very unlikely that these unfavorable conditions will persist for a great length of time.

Loss aversion also plays an important role here. When a company encounters problems that present the possibility of loss, people's natural tendency is to flee from the situation. Our natural inclination toward loss aversion, to avoid loss at almost any cost, will inevitably cause people to sell their positions in a company facing problems, virtually regardless of price. Thus, when a company is undergoing some short-term difficulty or trauma, people reflexively want to escape the situation, and they rarely stop to consider the price at which they are selling. Herd mentality is a further magnifying influence here. In fact, usually the selloff is so great that the resulting company is priced in the stock market as if it will take many years to recover, or will never recover. In some instances, a company that is undergoing a short-term yet solvable problem will be priced in the stock market below its liquidation value.

One fundamental aspect of true investing is heavily weighting the purchase price as a determinative factor in the desirability of an investment. This seems a relatively simple, straightforward and unassailable concept. People naturally consider price the most important factor in determining the suitability of an investment in most assets, whether it be a new car, a house, a farm, raw land, or an apartment building. In these privately negotiated transactions, the decision of whether to buy or sell is largely determined by a comparison of the price paid to the value received. Hence the value investing wisdom that a great asset can be a poor investment at too high a price, and a poor asset can be a great investment at a sufficiently low price.

However, in a very liquid public marketplace, the commonsense notion of price is in many instances trumped by the Foolishness of the

Crowd. In particular, when a company is facing problems and the potential for loss is present, uncertainty issues, loss aversion and herd mentality work together to cause people to engage in panicked selling. This panicked selling is for the most part divorced from price. In other words, during a crisis people do not stop and consider the value of the business they are selling relative to the price at which they are selling. Hence a situation where a company faces a short-term, solvable problem is a great candidate for mispricing for the patient investor.

One note of caution here is that when an investor identifies a situation where a company is encountering a short-term difficulty, the investor must rationally and logically appraise the situation and ensure that the problems facing the company are indeed short-term, i.e., that the problems are solvable and/or will very likely go away after a period of time. In other words, the investor must ensure that the company will remain viable as a going concern, that its business franchise is largely intact or will most certainly recover. In some instances, the problems a company is facing are neither short-term nor solvable, but rather the company has more fundamental problems in its business model. This is of particular concern in the area of technology companies, primarily because technology changes so quickly that it is difficult to predict with any certainty that a technology-focused business model will be viable well into the future.

Perhaps one of the most well-known examples of this issue was Warren Buffett's purchase of American Express Stock after the infamous "salad oil scandal." This scandal involved a white-collar crook by the name of Anthony de Angelis. Unable to obtain credit due to a prior bankruptcy, Angelis schemed to store containers ostensibly containing vegetable oil in a warehouse owned by a subsidiary of American Express. Angelis then used the American Express warehouse receipts as collateral for loans. One problem though was that the American Express warehouse containers in fact contained mostly seawater, with a thin layer of vegetable oil at the top. Thus Angelis was perpetrating a fraud on the American Express warehouse, all as a means to gain fake collateral for his loans. The second problem was that Angelis used the borrowed money to speculate on vegetable futures, and he ended up losing all of this money. When the creditors appeared at the warehouse to seize the collateral, the oil/seawater problem was discovered. The amount of the fraud was as much as $150 million by some estimates, enough to push the American Express subsidiary into bankruptcy. American Express' liability on these claims was uncertain, but the American Express CEO, rightfully recognizing that the reputation of the American Express brand was of prime importance, decided to take the moral high road, stating that "American Express Company feels morally bound . . . to see that such excess liabilities are satisfied." American Express was considered by many to be at risk of insolvency, and in a matter of days the stock dropped from its previous high of $60 to a low of $35 per share.

During this time the stock market was in a panic over the seeming demise of American Express, and the conventional wisdom was to sell the stock as fast as possible. Warren Buffett was watching these events with some interest, and he decided to conduct his own analysis and investigation into the effect of this scandal on the company. Buffett visited restaurants, banks, and travel agencies to confirm that American Express credit cards and traveler's checks were still being used as before. Buffett also visited supermarkets and drugstores to confirm that the purchase of American Express money orders was still business as usual. Buffett further talked to competitors to get their sense of how this scandal could affect American Express' business. Convinced that the American Express franchise was still intact and as strong as ever, Buffett invested approximately 25% of his partnership assets into American Express stock. Eventually the stock price rebounded, correcting the prior fear-induced overreaction, and the Buffett Partnership made a hefty profit on this investment.

Consider also the following examples. In the aftermath of the financial crisis of 2008-2009, in 2011 the stock prices of both Bank of

America and AIG reflected a value for these companies at well below liquidation value. However, one could fairly confidently assess that these companies' business models were enduring and that these companies would survive.

In the case of Bank of America, a dispassionate appraisal would reveal a company that did business with 1 out of every 2 to 3 Americans and which held over $1 trillion dollars of American deposits. Bank of America had essentially 5 different businesses, 4 of which were profitable, and one, mortgages, which was causing losses. However, the problems in its mortgage business were relatively short-term and solvable. The vast majority of bad loans were issued in 2008 and earlier. Given that the average life of a mortgage loan is around 7 years, many of these bad loan assets were starting to burn off. The loans made in 2009 and later were widely considered to be of high quality. It was certainly true that BofA's balance sheet was opaque in many respects, i.e., that it was difficult for investors to understand the nature of many of its assets and liabilities. Litigation expenses were also likely to last for some painful amount of time. However, with intelligent and rational analysis, one could relatively easily determine that BofA would not only survive, but that, given the powerful force of reversion to the mean, it was almost certain to return to its more normal earning power. Due to a combination of uncertainty, loss aversion, and herd mentality, as well as seeming outright hatred, Bank of America's stock price fell well below its liquidation value, and at some points in time less than half of its liquidation value. In other words, BofA was selling at fire-sale prices, and the courageous investor who could look past the doom and gloom to see a valuable banking franchise selling well below any measure of its intrinsic value was richly rewarded.

AIG was a storied insurance franchise, literally the 800 pound gorilla in international insurance, which had been brought to its knees via the actions of one small division in London. In particular, its London office had sold a large amount of credit protection, in the form of credit default swaps, on collateralized debt obligations (CDOs). These CDOs declined in value during the bursting of the housing bubble and the resulting financial crisis, placing AIG into a liquidity crisis. Ultimately the US Treasury and the Federal Reserve Bank of New York provided a total of over $180 billion dollars to fortify AIG's balance sheet and prevent its bankruptcy. After the bailouts AIG was literally the poster child of the financial crisis and was roundly hated by many in the market. However, a rational and dispassionate evaluation of AIG in 2011 would have revealed a somewhat slimmed down, but still large, insurance giant which was quickly buying back the government's interest, and which had an intact global insurance franchise that was on the path to return to profitability. However, the market was pricing AIG at below its liquidation value. An investor who had the courage to act at this time was richly rewarded.

Contrast this with two technology companies, Blackberry (previously Research in Motion) and Nokia. Blackberry and Nokia were the leaders in mobile phone sales in the mid-2000's, but rapidly lost market share to upstarts Apple and Android phones. Nokia was the world's largest vendor of mobile phones from 1998 through 2011, but its market share fell precipitously in 2012 – 2013, resulting in Nokia dropping from first to tenth in terms of market share. Similarly, Blackberry also saw its market share drop at a rapid pace. Thus, these two companies were clearly out of favor. However, the key question that should have been asked is whether the problems facing these two companies were both short-term and solvable. Here a carefully and thoroughly considered qualitative analysis of the smartphone business would have revealed that the problems facing these two companies were likely to be neither short-term, nor were they easily solvable. Or stated another way, the problems facing these two companies were not solvable to the degree of certainty required to warrant investment. Rather, there was a decent chance that the issues facing these two companies were likely to be systemic problems from which they were unlikely to recover. As this is written, Blackberry has failed in its attempt to sell itself and has undergone a recapitalization. Nokia has agreed to be purchased by Microsoft and will attempt its renaissance as a Microsoft subsidiary. Although the final chapter has yet to be written on either of these two companies, their future prospects seem dim. Even if one or both of these companies revives and returns to its former glory, the current facts and state of affairs render this potential future as sufficiently unlikely such that, at prices above liquidation value, there would be little or no margin of safety in the purchase. It is true that the stock of each of these companies may have been a bargain purchase at some point during this time, e.g., if / when the stock was selling well below the liquidation value of the company. For example, just as a great company can be a bad investment at too high of a price, a poor company can be a good investment at a sufficiently low price. However, one is not able to ascertain with any degree of confidence that there will be any upside from reversion to the mean in the cases of Blackberry and Nokia.

The Importance of Herd Mentality

As discussed above, one of the principal reasons the behavior of the crowd consensus causes stock market inefficiency is that the collective judgment of the crowd that a stock price is too high or too low causes an adjustment of the price to fully reflect this consensus opinion. In other words, once all of the members of the crowd who think the price is too high or too low register their votes, not only do these votes cause a corresponding change in the stock price, but in addition all of the crowd members who believe in this way will have voted, ultimately leaving no one left to further increase or decrease the price. In fact, at the time of such market extremes, when the pendulum has swung about as far as it will go, the only members of the crowd who remain to affect stock prices believe in the opposite thesis and hence are poised to return stock prices to a sense of normalcy. Thus we can see that the crowd's overreaction in driving stock prices in a particular direction sows the seed for movement of the stock price in the opposite direction. Or as explained by Howard Marks, the movement of the pendulum toward one extreme itself creates the causative factors for the pendulum's subsequent movement in the opposite direction.

Given the above, and considering our discussion of in favor and out of favor companies, clearly lack of independence / herd mentality is both a dominant and a magnifying influence in terms of stock mispricing. The propensity of the crowd to overreact in a herd-like manner is the primary cause of the corresponding overreaction in price. In other words, if a macro (or micro) economic problem or crisis occurs, causing the members of the crowd to vote on lower stock prices (i.e., causing a sell-off of stocks), the herd behavior will inevitably cause an overreaction, causing stock prices to become much lower than circumstances warrant. Here the investor can focus on companies whose stock price has suffered the most, or perhaps suffered the most needlessly, in reaction to the crisis. Similarly, if some short-term problems have beset a particular company, the market's myopic focus on short-term results coupled with herd mentality will tend to produce an overly exaggerated effect on the company's stock price.

Thus times of economic distress, when a particular company, or group of companies, is out of favor, can present terrific bargains to the value investor. However, the investor must convince himself that the respective company will survive with its business model sufficiently intact to return to its former standing. If a hitter in Major League Baseball is going through a slump, we can generally expect the hitter to eventually return to his normal batting average, but only if the player remains in the game. If the player suffers some type of permanent injury and is either dropped from the team or pushed down to the minor leagues, then he obviously will not be in a position to end his slump and return to his normal average. Thus here the powerful lesson is that reversion to the mean can only apply if the investor can stay in the game. If the investor can convince himself that the problems facing the company are both short-term and solvable, he can invest with the company and wait for the eventual turn-around. Here the investor can count on 1) the Foolishness of the Crowd to produce a bargain price; and 2) reversion of the mean to return both the company and its stock price to their former glory.

Final Thoughts

The third shortcut discussed above of identifying potential bargains based on knowledge of the Foolishness of the Crowd is currently practiced at least to a limited extent. One of the techniques of the value investing crowd is to seek out companies, or entire sectors, that are temporarily out of favor. One easy way to identify such companies is to search the stock pages for those companies hitting 52 week lows. Other value investors routinely scour various financial publications searching for companies that are undergoing short-term problems, or which are temporarily out of favor. If the investor can convince himself that the market has overreacted to the situation, and that the problems facing the company are both short-term and solvable, the investor can invest with the company and wait for the eventual turn-around.

One of the central goals of this book is to make the study of crowd wisdom criteria a more serious, more rigorous, and more useful area of study. More particularly, a central goal of this book is to produce a greater number of investors who: 1) become knowledgeable with regard to all of the different wisdom of the crowd criteria; 2) understand the interplay and reinforcement of the various different aspects of the Foolishness of the Crowd; 3) are actively on the lookout for when these criteria are observed to be lacking in the market; and 4) are ready to use this information as at least a partial basis for investment.

Of course the investor should also spend his time honing his skills as a value-based investor, becoming better at the various aspects of fundamental analysis, including accounting, financial statement analysis and developing an understanding of various businesses. However, given two equally competent investors, the one who in addition intentionally strives to focus on and take advantage of identifiably inefficient segments of the market will most likely be much more successful than the one who does not. The truth of the matter is that the stock market exhibits a large amount of efficiency, and stock prices will often be at least somewhat correct. Absent some criteria for identifying likely market inefficiencies, searching for mispriced securities in such an environment is very difficult, somewhat akin to searching for needles in the prover-bial haystack. For the intelligent investor who knows what to look for, i.e., who knows where the wisdom of the crowd is prone to falter, and is on the watch for such market inefficiencies, his search is much easier. In the analogy where the stock market is a haystack, it is almost as if the portions of the haystack where the needles reside are glowing, indicat-ing where the inefficiencies are occurring.

In summary, the fact that a large number of people participate in the stock market virtually guarantees that the Foolishness of the Crowd will be present when the relevant reasons or causative circumstances exist. In other words, if people were entirely rational and did not ex-hibit herd mentality, the wisdom of the crowd would likely prevail in producing correct stock prices, except for the relatively minor systemic constraints. However, given that people are decidedly not rational and do exhibit short-term thinking, herd mentality, etc. in their decision-making, the result of this irrationality and herd mentality is a "Foolish Offset" – an offset to the correct stock price produced by the Foolishness of the Crowd. This Foolish Offset is applied to the value that the wisdom of the crowd would have otherwise generated, producing mispriced se-curities. Here our understanding of when this Foolish Offset is pres-ent will help to identify potential mispricings in the stock market, and hence potential bargains. Next we will present an investment framework that is based on our understanding of the Foolishness of the Crowd.

7. THE VARIANT PERCEPTION AND THE INEFFICIENT RATIONALE

When the investor has identified some market inefficiency, he must have the courage to act and take a suitably large position. The size of his position will be based at least to some degree on the strength of his conviction. The investor must also possess the resolve to maintain his position despite the fact that it will likely be contrary to the sentiment of the crowd. First the investor must perform a fundamental analysis to estimate the intrinsic value of the business. There is simply no substitute for estimating the value of the business and insisting on a large margin of safety between your estimate of intrinsic value and the asking price of the stock. As a result of his valuation analysis, the investor will form a thesis for the mispricing of the stock, referred to as a "variant perception." The "variant perception" essentially represents the investor's thesis for his valuation of the stock, which will necessarily be different than the current consensus of the market. In addition, an understanding of the Foolishness of the Crowd can not only help in identifying where to search for bargains, it can also act as confirming evidence of mispricing. In other words, a proper understanding of the Foolishness of the Crowd can enable the investor to develop a rationale for why the market is mispricing the stock, i.e., why the crowd is not producing a wise or correct price. This rationale is referred to as the "inefficient rationale." In addition, social influence, normally the investor's worst enemy during times of irrational crowd behavior, can be turned around and used to the investor's direct advantage. The concepts of a variant perception, an inefficient rationale, and positive social influence are discussed below.

The Variant Perception

When the investor is considering a purchase during a time of individual security or overall market irrationality, it is critical that he make a dispassionate, rational estimation of the intrinsic value of the company in which he is considering investing. The investor must be firmly grounded in sound valuation principles and have some idea of the intrinsic values of the businesses he is considering through common stock purchases. When the stock prices fall well below these intrinsic value estimates, this should be the trigger point to buy. If the investor convinces himself that his estimation of the intrinsic value of a company is far greater than the current stock market price, and if there is little or no chance of serious impairment of that value as a result of current conditions, then the investor should have the fortitude to act, i.e., he should have the courage of his convictions. During periods of market irrationality, the investor should also periodically review any prior analysis he has made and make sure that significant facts or assumptions that he has relied upon have not changed.

In general, in order to make outsized gains in the stock market, the investor must 1) take positions that are contrary to the general consensus; and 2) these positions must be "correct" from a valuation and margin of safety standpoint. The first requirement above follows from the fact that if one invests in a manner that is largely consistent with the overall market, he will likely achieve only market returns. Thus generally the only way to achieve high returns in stock investments is to take positions that are different from the mainstream crowd. In other words, in order to make money investing, the investor must have a viewpoint that is different from the herd. For example, if an investor believes that a company is destined for considerable earnings growth in the foreseeable future, and everyone else in the market also shares that view, then this predicted growth is almost certainly factored into the current stock price. Thus if the company achieves the predicted earnings growth, the investor is still unlikely to make very much money on the stock. This is perhaps another way of saying that the market is quite often efficient, and thus making investments based on a thesis shared by the overall market is unlikely to produce outsized returns.

An investment thesis that is at odds with, or contrary to, the general market view or market consensus may be referred to as a "variant perception." This term was popularized by Michael Steinhardt, one of the most successful hedge fund managers of all time. In his book *No Bull— My Life In and Out of Markets*, Steinhardt noted:

> I told [a summer intern] that ideally he should be able to tell me in two minutes, four things: 1- the idea; 2- the consensus view; 3- his variant perception; and 4- a trigger event. No mean feat. In those instances where there was no variant perception – that is, solid growth recommendations within consensus – I generally had no interest and would discourage investing.[37]

Steinhardt required not only that the analyst present an idea with a logically sound thesis, but that the idea itself had to be different from the consensus view of the market. Thus a question that the investor should ask himself before investing is "What do I understand or believe about this company that is different from the mainstream view?" In other words, before making an investment, the investor should be able to identify a variant perception or contrarian view about the company and its prospects that is different from the consensus or market view.

Taking contrary positions is generally easy – the hard part is identifying a contrary position that is correct. Steinhardt himself defined the term "variant perception" as "holding a *well-founded* view that was meaningfully different from market consensus," and he often said that "the only analytical tool that mattered was an *intellectually advantaged* disparate view (emphasis added)."[38] Again, the fact is that the stock market is often quite efficient, and in many instances the crowd is largely right. Thus the key to investing lies in the ability to identify *correct* investment theses that are contrary to the consensus view. Again in the words of Michael Steinhardt:

> To be a contrarian is easy, but to be contrarian and to be right in your judgment when the consensus is wrong is where you get the golden ring and it doesn't happen that much, but when it does happen you make extraordinary amounts of money.[39]

The Inefficient Rationale

Having a variant perception, an intelligent and well-informed contrary viewpoint to that of the crowd, is certainly important to successful investing. However, we would go further and argue that having an understanding of *why* the crowd is incorrect is also extremely important, perhaps more important. One of the most important and helpful things to an investor is the knowledge of exactly *why* the market is behaving as it is, e.g., why an individual company, or the entire market, is being offered for sale at absurdly low or high prices. In other words, the investor should be able to articulate a rationale as to why the consensus view is incorrect, i.e., why the wisdom of the crowd is not present in this situation. Here we develop the concept of the "Inefficient Rationale" – the investor's articulated explanation as to why crowd wisdom is not generating a correct price, i.e., why the overall market is producing an incorrect price (or prices).

In formulating a variant perception about a company's valuation, we previously counseled the investor to ask: "What do I understand or believe about this company that is different from the mainstream view?" The next question the investor should ask is: "Based on my understanding of the wisdom of the crowd, and in particular my understanding of the criteria necessary for the wisdom of the crowd to be applicable, what is the explanation as to why the crowd wisdom is incorrect – why is the market mispricing this stock?" At the beginning of Section 2 we quoted from Sir John Templeton: "If you're going to buy the best bargains, you have to buy the things that people are selling." The inefficient rationale is essentially the explanation, based on lack of one or more crowd wisdom criteria, as to why market participants are selling *for reasons other than price.* If market participants are selling a stock because it is currently overpriced, this is obviously not of interest to the investor. The inefficient rationale seeks to explain why participants are selling a stock that the investor believes is underpriced, i.e., a stock for which the investor has a variant perception.

Thus the investor should seek an explanation or rationale, most likely grounded in some combination of the market's behavioral psychology and/or systemic market inefficiencies, as to why the market is producing an incorrect price. Recall our discussion above regarding the "Foolish Offset" from the wisdom of the crowd. The inefficient rationale is the explanation for this Foolish Offset. Hence, in addition to developing a well-founded viewpoint or thesis that is the contrary to the mainstream crowd (the variant perception), the investor should also develop a rationale or thesis, typically from a psychological standpoint, as to *why* the mainstream crowd is wrong (the inefficient rationale). Armed with this rationale as to why the wisdom of the crowd is not reflected in the current stock price, the investor is better able to identify or confirm such mispricings and is poised to act with conviction when such mispricings are identified.

The "Inefficient Rationale" is thus an intellectually sound explanation, based on our newfound understanding of the applicability requirements of the wisdom of the crowd, as to why the prevailing consensus view is incorrect. Without such an explanation or rationale, the investor is likely to wonder how the market, the crowd, could be so wrong. After all, the wisdom of the crowd is a powerful force. As we saw in Chapters 1-3, when certain criteria are present the wisdom of the crowd will be largely manifest in stock prices. If the investor does not have a clear understanding of why the crowd might be wrong in this instance, then he should be extremely cautious, as he may be going against a truly wise crowd.

For many investors, reliance solely on valuation principles and estimates of intrinsic value at times will simply not be sufficient. For example, when the stock market is declining rapidly and fear and panic are widely prevalent, there is great temptation from both an intellectual and psychological standpoint to believe that the crowd may be right. At best, the investor will inevitably begin to doubt his valuations, and even a small amount of doubt can lead to inaction or, even worse, panicked selling. During this time a number of psychological forces are acting in concert telling you to sell rather than buy. When the stock market is advancing rapidly, and optimism / euphoria prevail, there will be great temptation to join the crowd in purchasing overpriced securities. Thus some additional confidence may be needed to help ensure he is capable of making the right decisions during periods of market folly. The investor must not only have the resolve to commit capital to positions that he has identified as mispriced, but he must also have the resolve to maintain his positions even when the herd is moving in the opposite direction. Further, the investor must have the fortitude to avoid jumping into a frothy market and buying overpriced securities.

Thus, during times of market irrationality, if the investor does not have an understanding of how this abnormal crowd behavior produces a Foolish Offset from the normal wisdom of the crowd, the investor will be apt to presume that his estimations of value are incorrect. In other words, without any alternative explanation of the market's strange behavior, the investor is very likely to doubt the correctness of his views, and this doubt will inevitably lead to inaction, or worse, incorrect action. Therefore, if the investor does not have a good rationale as to why the crowd is collectively offering absurd, even foolish, prices, he is more likely to presume that the crowd is right and he is wrong, and he is unlikely to have sufficient confidence to go against the crowd. This is where having both the right temperament and a thorough understanding of market psychology is critical. An understanding of the psychological basis and incentives for people's actions in the stock market will give the investor a more complete picture as to why the market is behaving irrationally with respect to valuation and pricing. More importantly, this knowledge will allow him to correctly rely on psychological irrationality as the basis for market mispricing, instead of simply presuming that his valuation estimates are grossly incorrect. Stated more clearly, when the market is presenting prices that are out of line with the investor's own views of valuation, the informed investor will often be able to cite the Foolishness of the Crowd as the underlying reason. The Foolishness of the Crowd will become his inefficient rationale. Armed with an understanding of the various behavioral and psychological forces at play, the investor can observe these forces in action as an inefficient rationale that provides the needed confirmation for his variant perception. In other words, now that the investor understands the causes of irrationality, the investor can become more attuned to evidence confirming that the causes of this irrationality are present in the market. Once the investor understands that crowd irrationality, the Foolishness of the Crowd, is the cause of these bargain prices, he has much less reason to doubt his own analysis, and he can then act with much greater confidence. This topic is discussed in more detail below with respect to both macroeconomic and microeconomic foolishness.

Much like an investor can have varying levels of conviction in a valuation thesis (or variant perception), an inefficient rationale can be either weak, moderate, or strong, depending on the crowd psychology or systemic forces that form its underlying basis. In other words, certain Foolishness of the Crowd phenomena when present alone tend to produce a potentially weak inefficient rationale, while others tend to produce a much stronger inefficient rationale. As discussed above, certain wisdom of the crowd criteria seem to be always lacking in the stock market, while others are much more pronounced during different points in the market cycle. For example, short-term thinking is seemingly always present in the market, regardless of where the market pendulum is positioned in the current cycle. Thus the propensity for market participants to exhibit short-term thinking that seems divorced from the long-term prospects of the underlying business is seemingly always a potential inefficient rationale. However, when such short-term thinking forms the sole basis for the inefficient rationale, then, while likely valid, the inefficient rationale should be carefully considered for its relative strength. Potential systemic constraints that could form the basis for an inefficient rationale are a company's (small) size, its lack of presence or under-representation in indexes or ETFs, its presence in a particular out of favor index, the company having been the subject of a recent spinoff, and other possible systemic inefficiencies. The presence of one or more of these systemic constraints adds additional strength to the inefficient rationale. When the inefficient rationale is at least partly based on elements of irrational crowd psychology and herd behavior, such as fear or greed, the inefficient rationale may be seen as particularly strong. In general, most of the greatest investments have been due to the presence of a strong inefficient rationale, usually the presence of fear and uncertainty in the market place. In the words of Sir John Templeton, most of the greatest investments have been made at the "time of maximum pessimism." Most value investors would easily agree that times of extreme market fear and panic provide the most fertile ground for outstanding investments. Finally, various different types of crowd foolishness and/or systemic constraints can often combine together or work in concert to create a lollapalooza effect of market inefficiency that is greater than merely the sum of its parts.

Variant Perception and No Inefficient Rationale

For some type of potential investments, the investor's fundamental analysis may lead him to a variant perception that is different from the market consensus. However, the investor may not be able to identify a strong inefficient rationale as to why the market is mispricing the stock. Without such an inefficient rationale, the investor is left to conclude that, based on publicly available information, the crowd is simply reaching a less correct conclusion, or that the investor has somehow reached a more correct conclusion than the market, i.e., the investor is wiser than the crowd. Here the investor should tread very carefully. When the appropriate criteria are present, the crowd can be very wise, and absent a compelling explanation as to why the wisdom of the crowd is not applicable in this situation, it can be dangerous to bet against the crowd's wisdom. When such an inefficient rationale is not present, or is present to only a weak degree, the investor should recheck his analysis and think very carefully about the merits of the investment. It would seemingly be very difficult to have high conviction in an investment where there was no strong inefficient rationale clearly explaining the crowd's error in judgment.

One of the greatest dangers for the successful investor is the failure to fully appreciate the importance of an inefficient rationale, and hence the failure to distinguish between investment situations when such a rationale exists, and when it does not. Consider the following situation which through experience can be observed fairly often. A good investor may have a string of successful investments where for each successful investment there was in fact a clear and strong inefficient rationale for the mispricing, although the investor did not fully recognize it or appreciate its importance. When a new investment opportunity presents itself that based on the investor's fundamental analysis appears to have a large margin of safety, but which does not have a strong inefficient rationale, the investor may be lulled into a false sense of security based on his past successes. Due to some combination of past success, overconfidence, and hubris, the investor may come to believe himself truly smarter than the crowd. However, if the investor does not understand the circumstances necessary for the wisdom of the crowd to be present, and hence is not able to differentiate when this wisdom is and is not present, he is asking for trouble. In short, where the investor does not realize the conditions that cause a "Foolish Offset" from the normal wisdom of the crowd, or does not fully appreciate the importance of a Foolish Offset as an indicator of mispricing, he may fail to take extra caution when this offset is not present.

Inefficient Rationale and No Variant Perception

For other types of potential investments, the investor may observe irrational market behavior that he believes surely should produce irrational pricing for one or more stocks. However, the investor's fundamental analysis may not lead him to a markedly different valuation than the current consensus. In this instance, the investor will not be able to formulate a variant perception of valuation of the stock that is different from the market consensus. In this situation we would urge the investor to re-check his fundamental analysis. If current economic conditions are somewhat abnormal, then the investor should consider forming a valuation estimate of the company assuming a more normal economic environment. More specifically, the investor should attempt to estimate the earnings power of the business that would exist in a more normal economic environment, and estimate a valuation of the business based on this earning power. As noted above, here it is critical that the investor ensure that the business franchise will survive any short-term economic troubles. If the investor is fairly confident that the business will survive, then he can generally count on reversion to the mean to enable the company to return to its average earning power.

The presence of an inefficient rationale – of clearly identifiable market irrationality – is likely a better predictor of mispricing than any individual's estimate of value based on fundamental analysis. In one sense, the wisdom of the crowd can be viewed as always present, where some times this wisdom is offset by crowd irrationality (Foolishness) and other times it is not, i.e., sometimes a Foolish Offset is applied to this otherwise wise result, and at other times no Foolish Offset is present. When conditions are present that clearly indicate that the wisdom of the crowd will NOT be reflected in stock prices, i.e., where it is clear that some type of Foolish Offset is present to shift stock prices away from their correct prices, it is very likely that a mispricing will occur. This evidence of mispricing can, and perhaps should, be more compelling than the investor's estimate of value. Here it is tempting to advocate that an investor purchase a stock based solely on his inefficient rationale – his identification of market irrationality – even though he is unable to form a corresponding variant perception, i.e., even though his own valuation estimates do not seem to indicate a mispricing. One approach is that, when crowd irrationality is affecting a number of different companies, and where the investor is not able to confirm his inefficient rationale's evidence of mispricing with his own valuation estimate for any single company, he should consider buying a basket of such likely mispriced stocks. Recall that Benjamin Graham, the father of security analysis, recommended that an investor purchase a basket of net-net stocks based purely on a somewhat limited quantitative analysis, without doing any fundamental valuation based on an understanding of the business and its long-term prospects. A similar strategy based on the principles of this book would be to buy a basket of stocks for which there is a clear inefficient rationale, again without the requirement of any rigorous supporting fundamental business valuation analysis. The premise would be that a large number, if not all, of these companies would be underpriced based merely on the knowledge that some type of foolish irrationality is present in the marketplace.

Using Social Influence to Your Advantage – The Wisdom of a Select Crowd

We learned above that social influence is a powerful force in directing our behavior and actions. The term "social influence" refers to the fact that people generally take cues from others in how to conduct their behavior. This is often a very useful mental shortcut, as in many instances there is wisdom from the crowd, and emulating the behavior of others is often the right thing to do. However, as we have seen, crowd behavior in a financial marketplace can sometimes be foolish, not wise, and following the herd can lead to riding over the cliff with everyone else. Herd mentality is perhaps the strongest psychological influence in the stock market. Therefore, the ability to stay detached from the crowd during times of foolishness is perhaps the most important attribute of the successful investor.

Here it is critical that the investor turn what would normally be one of his biggest disadvantages, the influence of the irrational crowd, into perhaps one of his greatest advantages. The way to turn social influence to your advantage is by *selecting a smaller, more intelligent crowd to join and follow.* More specifically, the investor should select and join a crowd that believes in the same value investing principles, and optimally has at least a partial understanding of the nature of the Foolishness of the Crowd. One way to accomplish this is by developing friends and acquaintances who share the same value investing mind-set. During times of market irrationality, these friends can provide a wealth of support. In addition, there are a number of value investing online forums and boards that an investor can join (mentioned previously), with intelligent discussion of current investing topics from the standpoint of value investing principles. During a macroeconomic crisis and a resulting large market decline, the investor will be able to read intelligent commentary from others about the foolishness of the market, and even more importantly will be able to correspond and interact with others who are actively buying securities. Similarly, during a stock market bubble when stock prices are outrunning business valuations, the investor will be able to interact with others who are selling stocks or are sitting on the sidelines waiting for the inevitable return to rational prices. Such forums can be a huge support network for the investor, providing constant reminder that the investor is not the "only one" who is going against the mainstream.

The investor should also follow the actions and commentary of the great value investors during times of irrationality. As noted above, investment funds are required to report their recent securities acquisitions every quarter in a 13-F filing. Thus during a lengthy market decline the investor is able to follow and compare what the great investors have bought. Similarly, during a market advance the investor is able to determine what the great investors are selling. In addition, many of the great investors will often appear on television and in interviews trumpeting their recent stock purchases, or short position theses, explaining the rationales and theories on certain investments. The thoughts and decisions of these great investors should of course be viewed with a critical, skeptical eye, but time spent following great investors who are buying during a downturn, instead of listening to the conventional financial news, is much more likely to be fattening to the pocketbook. In particular, during a time of market distress, if a particular sector (e.g., financials) is being affected by the crisis, the investor may be able to seek out value-based fund managers who have expertise in that sector. During times of market euphoria, the investor will be able to derive comfort from various other prominent value investors who are not caught up in the hysteria, and hence are not buying the overvalued stocks being offered for sale.

Thus the investor can gain the benefit of the true wisdom of an intelligent crowd – the wisdom of a smaller value investing crowd which understands: a) fundamental valuation (and hence is able to formulate an intelligent variant perception) and b) the criteria for market inefficiencies (and hence is able to formulate an inefficient rationale). Unlike the mainstream crowd, such a value-investing crowd will generally not suffer from any type of Foolish Offset that would obscure its wisdom. In fact, as described above, some of the most successful value investors, most notably Mohnish Pabrai, have advocated "cloning", or copying the investing decisions of other great investors. This cloning strategy has usually involved surveying the investment decisions of other respected value investors, and selecting a subset of those that make sense on a fundamental valuation basis to the investor. This cloning strategy should also include giving greater weight to investment ideas that are well supported by respected value investors. In other words, the more that this wise crowd supports an investment idea, the more credence the investor should likely give to this idea. In this regard, a valuable service would be to track the investment decisions of a small universe of respected value investors and rank their investments based on the number of value investors supporting each investment. Such a ranking could also conceivably use different weightings for different value investors, based on their perceived expertise or prior records. This would provide a mechanism to truly take advantage of the wisdom of this select crowd.

The investor should also attempt to "tune out" as much of the conventional crowd noise as possible. This does not mean that the investor should stick his head in the sand and ignore various economic and market developments. Far from it, the investor needs to stay apprised with what is happening, mostly to make sure he is as fully aware as possible of all of the potential bargains. However, the investor should generally limit his exposure to the various talking heads on financial television channels preaching either doom and gloom or euphoria. The primary goal of any television show is to turn a profit, primarily by attracting as much viewership as possible. This is often down by overdoing and over dramatizing any significant event, portraying every somewhat significant macro event either as a crisis or a "golden opportunity." Thus the investor should view conventional financial news with a heavy dose of skepticism, and he should attempt to glean factual developments from conventional financial news while not getting caught up in the hysteria.

In addition, to the extent that the investor pays attention to the mainstream media during times of stock market folly, he should actively seek out confirming evidence of market irrationality. This evidence will likely be widely prevalent. The investor's observations of market irrationality will provide him a measure of comfort in his contrarian views. The investor's deliberate efforts to join and follow, and hence be influenced by, a wiser crowd can be seen as "positive social influence" – the investor is attempting to benefit from the positive influence of a wise crowd. In turn, the investor's deliberate efforts to identify and realize the Foolishness on the part of the large speculative crowd can be used as a form of "negative social influence". The term "negative social influence" is used to refer to a person observing the foolish actions of a crowd that he knows to be "unwise," and using this knowledge and understanding of foolishness to buttress his desire to avoid this crowd behavior as well as take positions contrary to the unwise crowd. Thus the investor is observing crowd behavior in the market that he understands to be clearly foolish, and he is using this observation as a means to reassure himself that: 1) he should NOT emulate this larger crowd; and 2) he likely should be taking positions that are contrary to the crowd. Knowledge of the root causes of this foolishness (the inefficient rationale) is very important, as such knowledge allows the investor to recognize this foolishness as such. With both understanding and observation of this crowd irrationality, the investor will be able to view the actions of the foolish crowd as the folly that it is, and he will want to disassociate himself from it. Therefore, just as social influence from a truly wise crowd can be a source of great comfort and assurance, informed observations of a foolish crowd can provide a similar level of assurance of the undesirability of following such an unwise crowd. This aspect of "negative social influence" can serve as the basis for the variant perception discussed above.

When the investor's only crowd association is the mainstream public, taking the correct contrarian positions can be exceedingly difficult. By choosing to become an active member of a smaller, like-minded crowd, the investor can actually make the strong psychological principle of social influence work in his favor. A combination of like-minded friends, a value-based Internet community, and following the great value investors can do wonders for the investor's resolve during times of extreme market irrationality. In addition, armed with knowledge of the psychology of misjudgment, the investor is in a position to view the crowd's irrational behavior for what it is. This will actually be a source of comfort, as repeated observations of clearly identifiable crowd foolishness will cause him to actively shun emulation of the larger crowd.

It is important to note that, despite the admonition above to consort with like-minded investors, it is critically important that the investor not completely ignore the mainstream (consensus) view. In fact, he should be able to articulate the consensus view at least as well as its most ardent proponents. The investor should be able to articulate both the consensus view and his variant perception, and make a decision between the two based on an application of rational intelligence and valuation as well as on his inefficient rationale – a clear understanding of the behavioral psychology affecting the market.

High Conviction Investments

In our opinion, the best, highest conviction investments that can be made arise when: 1) the investor has performed a fundamental valuation analysis which reveals that the company has a valuation significantly higher than its selling price (a large margin of safety), thus enabling the investor to form a strong variant perception about the company's value which differs from the current consensus; and 2) the investor is able to postulate a strong "inefficient rationale" for this mispricing – a rationale that is based on identifiable crowd irrationality or other market inefficiency that prevents the wisdom of the crowd from producing the correct price; and 3) "wise social influence" is present, i.e., other seasoned and similar minded value investors are piling into the investment (and ideally the price has dropped further since these other great investors began buying). When the investor, based on his fundamental analysis, is able to formulate an intelligent variant perception that is different than the market consensus, and in addition is able to develop an understanding of an inefficient rationale as to why the market is producing this incorrect price, the odds will be very good that the investment is a sound one. When the investor can further observe other intelligent value investors applying a similar analysis and reaching the same conclusion, the odds of this being a quality investment are even greater.

It is important to note that each of the "inefficient rationale" and the presence of "wise social influence" are derived from crowd-based principles. Obviously, wise social influence draws directly from the principle of the wisdom of the crowd, being based as it is on the decisions of intelligent, rational value-based investors who are collectively producing a wise result. Thus wise social influence is a product of the wisdom of the crowd in its purest form. The inefficient rationale is also based on a form of the wisdom of the crowd. The inefficient rationale is based on the fact that *normally* the wisdom of the crowd produces correct prices, but *most importantly* is also based on the reliability of irrational crowd behavior in producing an offset from this normally wise price under certain conditions. This reliable crowd behavior when certain "wisdom of the crowd" criteria are absent is what guarantees the resultant mispricing.

Thus we can view the variant perception, inefficient rationale, and wise social influence as three supporting legs of a great investment. When each of these legs is present to a large degree, then the investment has a solid foundation, and a strong case can be made for the investment. In this case, the investment idea is likely to be one of high conviction, deserving of a large position in the portfolio. As any one of these legs weakens, the merit of the proposed investment also likely weakens as well. For example, consider where the investor has: 1) a somewhat weak variant perception; 2) a strong case for an inefficient rationale; and 3) presence of wise social influence. This scenario can still merit a substantial investment, although understandably this would not be as high of conviction as where all three legs were equally strong. Next consider a scenario where the investor has: 1) a strong variant perception; 2) a weak case for an inefficient rationale; and 3) mild presence of wise social influence. This scenario can still merit investment, although this would perhaps be the same or less level of conviction than the previous one.

When only two of these legs are present, there will necessarily be less conviction in the idea. Here the amount of conviction would depend on which two legs are present. We would argue that investor's variant perception and inefficient rationale are the most important, with wise social influence a not-so distant third. The investor's intelligent variant perception is seemingly the most important, as the investor ideally should have a well-reasoned thesis about his investment. However, his inefficient rationale is oftentimes equally important, and in some instances can perhaps be even more important depending on the degree of crowd irrationality that is present. We realize that many value investors would disagree with the above statement, arguing that their studied analysis of an investment – their variant perception – trumps any guidance that can be obtained from the crowd. However, the reliability of crowd behavior under certain conditions, particularly extreme periods of fear and greed, is extremely powerful. In short, under some circumstances the reliability of crowd misbehavior can be a stronger indication of a good investment than any single investor's studied analysis.

In formulating a framework for investment, the investor will inevitably weight the relative importance of each of these legs in his overall decision-making process. Having done so, for each particular investment opportunity the investor will assess the strength of each of his supporting legs. Although different investors will understandably weight each of these legs slightly differently, it is critical that each of these legs, and in particular the variant perception and the inefficient rationale, be fully considered for optimum investment results. The variant perception (the investor's valuation thesis that is different from the market) and the inefficient rationale (the understanding of crowd irrationality and/or systemic forces that are producing this mispricing) are the main supporting legs of an investment, and can be considered the primary tools in the investor's toolkit. Unless you are one of those rare investment geniuses such as Warren Buffett or Charlie Munger, who have no need to copy other's investments (and in fact they are the ones who are usually copied), wise social influence should also be part of your investing toolkit.

8. INVESTMENT CASE STUDIES - THE VARIANT PERCEPTION AND THE INEFFICIENT RATIONALE

The following is a discussion of some example investments which involve either: 1) both a variant perception and a strong inefficient rationale; or 2) a variant perception and a weak or non-existent inefficient rationale. By contrasting different investments that had varying degrees of an inefficient rationale, we hope to illustrate the importance of selecting investments where there is a clear and strong inefficient rationale. The presence of such a rationale, based as it is largely on an appreciation of the reliability of crowd behavior and psychology, provides a clear and understandable reason as to why a stock is mispriced. In our opinion, the presence of a strong inefficient rationale can many times be the best and most reliable guidepost for a good investment.

Variant Perception and Inefficient Rationale

The following are some examples of investments which involved both a variant perception and a strong accompanying inefficient rationale. These investments hopefully can be used to illustrate a thought process for better investment decision-making.

1. American Express – Salad Oil Scandal

Warren Buffett's purchase of American Express stock described in Chapter 6 is a good example of an investment decision that involved both a variant perception and an inefficient rationale. Recall that a subsidiary of American Express had been caught up in a large scandal, having issued warehouse receipts for nonexistent salad oil, where these receipts were later used as collateral for large loans that were ultimately defaulted. Thus American Express was potentially on the hook for tens of millions of dollars.

The mainstream view was that American Express was in serious financial trouble, that the losses from the discovered fraud could possibly bankrupt the company. Hence the crowd voted a much lower price for American Express stock. Buffett's variant perception was that the monetary loss that American Express was likely to suffer would not bankrupt the company, but rather the American Express business franchise was intact and would fully recover. In fact, Buffett commented at the time that the money American Express was offering to settle the claims could more intelligently be viewed as "a dividend check that got lost in the mail." As previously discussed, in forming his variant perception, Buffett visited a number of businesses where American Express products were used to convince himself that American Express' business franchise was intact. Once Buffett was convinced that the business of American Express was sound, he could in some sense rely on the powerful force of reversion to the mean to return both the company and the stock to a sense of normalcy.

Buffett, who understood the foolishness of markets perhaps as well as anyone, also very likely developed his own "inefficient rationale" as well. His inefficient rationale would probably have been based on his understanding and experience that the market had a tendency to overreact to bad news. With recent insights from psychology and behavioral finance, we can elaborate somewhat on this inefficient rationale as being an overreaction due to a combination of loss aversion, problems with uncertainty and outright fear. More specifically, here the inefficient rationale would have been that the manner in which people (poorly) handle negative uncertainty would also have caused a large overreaction. In addition, fear from the shock of such a large scandal would have caused general panic in the market for American Express stock. Loss aversion, which refers to people's irrationally strong tendency to avoid loss at any cost, and now driven by fear of further loss, would have also played a major factor in a selloff. During a time of uncertainty and fear, most people have great difficulty envisioning normal, more placid times. Loss aversion, fear and uncertainty are powerful forces in their own right, but combined together they are especially potent.

Thus, to summarize, the consensus view, the variant perception, and the inefficient rationale would have been as follows:

Consensus view: American Express is in serious financial trouble due to the scandal, and could possibly go bankrupt. The future of the company is uncertain, and there is potential for loss. Hence the stock price should be severely discounted until this uncertainty is removed.

Variant perception: The business franchise of American Express is intact. People are still using American Express cards, checks and other services as they have before. The company may suffer some financial loss from the scandal, but its overall business is sound. Further, the company has the financial resources to weather this storm, and will return to a more normal state once the uncertainty is gone. Assuming that American Express weathers this temporary storm, its valuation is far greater than the current stock price.

Inefficient Rationale: Most in the market are engaged in short-term thinking, thus preventing participants from envisioning American Express returning to a more normal environment. Also, the market is experiencing a combination of uncertainty, fear, and loss aversion, which is causing the market to behave irrationally. Herd mentality is operating as a further magnifying influence. Hence the stock is temporarily extremely mispriced.

Warren Buffett profited handsomely from his American Express investment. Due to the scandal, American Express stock had dropped from $60 per share in November of 1963 to a low of $35 per share in early 1964. Unknown to his limited partners, Buffett invested 25% of his partnership fund into this single stock – shares that Berkshire Hathaway still owns as of 2014, 50 years later. By 1965, less than year later, American Express stock had hit $73, more than doubling from its low.

2. Johnson & Johnson – Tylenol Poisoning Scare

Johnson & Johnson is a large multinational corporation with products in a number of different areas such as consumer goods, medical devices and pharmaceuticals. One of its products is a pain reliever sold under the brand name Tylenol. In 1982 several bottles of Tylenol in the Chicago ago area were tampered with, wherein someone introduced poison into the capsules, resulting in seven deaths. After news reports that several people had died from consuming Tylenol laced with poison, the stock price of Johnson & Johnson declined by almost 30%, and the market value of the company declined by $1 billion. Interestingly, a number of other firms in the industry also suffered marked share price declines as a fallout over the uncertainty of new packaging regulations and their effect on the industry.

Here the consensus view was that this tragedy would do irreparable damage to J&J, and that the Tylenol brand itself was all but dead. At the time, Tylenol accounted for approximately 15% of the company's net income, which was very significant to the company. After reports of the tragedy, Tylenol's share of the $1.2 billion analgesic market quickly plunged from around 37% to 7%. Marketers and news pundits confidently predicted at the time that the Tylenol brand would never recover from the sabotage. There was no precedent to a situation such as this, where a product sold on store shelves had been modified to kill its purchasers. Thus there was great uncertainty about the future of Johnson & Johnson.

From an investment standpoint, the variant perception would have focused on the long-term earnings power and value of the corporation, especially in light of steps immediately taken to address the problem. Tylenol accounted for around 15% of J&J's income, but yet the stock price had already declined almost 30%. Thus clearly there was an overreaction to the tragedy. In other words, the company was being valued as if the entire Tylenol product line had permanently disappeared and the company was certain to suffer further earnings loss as well. In addition, immediately after the tragedy came to light, Johnson & Johnson executives acted quickly and decisively to avert further damage to the brand and the company itself. First and most importantly, they began taking the proper and necessary steps designed to safeguard consumers from further potential harm. Soon after learning of the issue, J&J recalled 31 million bottles of Tylenol capsules from store shelves and offered replacement product in the safer tablet form free of charge. Thus, J&J ordered a full recall of Tylenol products across the country, not just in the state where the tampering was known to have occurred. The company also decided to not re-establish the product on store shelves until it had come up with a solution that provided better product protection. Certainly these steps had significant near-term costs, but it was heartening to an investor that J&J was placing more importance on the long-term value of the brand over current profits. Thus the variant perception was that the company was likely more valuable than the current stock price even if the Tylenol brand ceased to exist. Further, if the Tylenol brand recovered even some semblance of its former stature, then the company would be worth considerably more than its current selling price.

As with the American Express example above, the inefficient rationale would have been at least partly based on the notion that, for a number of reasons, the market has a tendency to overreact to bad news. More particularly, the inefficient rationale would have included a combination of problems with uncertainty, fear and loss aversion. As noted above, an incident such as this had never occurred, and up to that time there had never been a product recall even close to the magnitude proposed by J&J. During a time of such uncertainty and fear, most participants would not have been able to envision the Tylenol brand returning to normalcy. Thus the mishandling of negative uncertainty, outright fear, and extreme loss aversion would have produced a lollapalooza effect of emotional over-reaction. This was actually on display in the market, as the stock seesawed in panic selling. Observation of this market panic would have added confirmation to the inefficient rationale.

Thus, to summarize, the consensus view, the variant perception, and the inefficient rationale would have been as follows:

Consensus view: Johnson & Johnson has a serious public relations problem, and people may be understandably reluctant to buy any J&J product. The Tylenol brand is almost certainly dead, and Tylenol was a significant revenue / profit generator for the company. There is a tremendous amount of fear and uncertainty around not only Tylenol, but also the company itself. The company is obviously worth much less today than it was a week ago. Hence the stock price should be severely discounted to reflect the loss of this product brand and its associated income, and also to reflect the uncertainty surrounding the company.

Variant perception: Johnson & Johnson is a large diverse company with many different brands and products. The company will suffer some financial loss from the tragedy, but it is taking the right steps to address the situation and maintain consumer confidence. For example, company management announced a full product recall and is being honest and forthright in dealing with the media. Although the Tylenol brand has certainly suffered temporary damage, people have a tendency to forget the past, and hence the brand will likely recover at least some of its former strength. This incident has not reduced the value of Johnson & Johnson by 30%, and thus the stock price will eventually recover.

Inefficient Rationale: The poisoning tragedy has caused a lot of fear and uncertainty in the minds of both consumers and investors alike. The market is thus experiencing a combination of fear, uncertainty, and loss aversion, which is causing the market to price J&J irrationally low. Also, market participants are focused on the crisis of the moment, and they are extrapolating the current conditions well out into the future. In other words, many in the market are engaged in short-term thinking, thus preventing them from envisioning Johnson & Johnson operating in a more normal environment once the current crisis has passed. Herd mentality is operating as a further magnifying influence. Hence the stock is temporarily extremely mispriced.

The bold investor who bought J&J stock soon after the crisis was richly rewarded. As noted above, many predicted that the Tylenol brand would never recover. But only two months later, Tylenol was back on store shelves, now in tamper-proof packaging and bolstered by an extensive media campaign. A year later, its share of the $1.2 billion analgesic market, which had plunged from 37 percent to 7 percent following the poisoning, had climbed back to 30 percent.

The stock price, which was the subject of panic selling, and which had dropped 30% immediately after the scare, recovered to its previous high only two months later. In fact, if an investor had purchased $1,000 in Johnson & Johnson stock on September 28, 1982, just *before* the first Tylenol episode, 20 years later, in 2002, he would have had $22,062.

3. Bank of America and Wells Fargo – 2008 Sub-Prime Mortgage Crisis

The financial crisis of 2008-9 produced bargains in virtually all corners of the market. However, perhaps the greatest bargains to be found were in the financial institutions, which were at the very center of the storm. Here we will examine the consensus view, variant perception, and inefficient rationale for each of Bank of America (BAC) and Wells Fargo (WFC) during this time period, although note that we could substitute the name of virtually any bank or financial institution, or virtually any company for that matter, into this analysis. Among all of the large US banks, Bank of America was perhaps the poster child for the financial crisis and resulting bailout. In a few short months Bank of America stock dropped from a high of over $37 per share in September 2008 (and a previous year's high of $52 per share) to a little over $3 per share in March 2009. Wells Fargo dropped from a prior high of close to $40 per share in September 2008 to a low of little over $8 per share in March 2009.

During the height of the financial crisis, the consensus view seemed to be that utter financial catastrophe was at hand, threatening the entire economy, and that financial institutions in particular were in serious threat of insolvency. This was not an entirely irrational viewpoint, given the recent bankruptcies of Bear Stearns and Lehman Brothers. Thus the consensus view was that banks were valued as if insolvency were a near certainty, and even then their valuations were much less than tangible book value, which can be considered a rough proxy for liquidation value. The variant perception was that the Too Big To Fail (TBTF) banks would mostly likely survive the financial crisis, and that in particular the government would step in and do whatever was needed to prevent financial Armageddon. Thus the variant perception was that eventually conditions would return to something approaching normal, and the large banks would correspondingly return to a more normal earnings environment. A part of the variant perception was also that, assuming a somewhat reasonable worst case, the large banks were at least worth their liquidation values, or a significant fraction thereof. Since at the time the stock market was valuing these two large banks at much less than their liquidation values, there was a considerable margin of safety in the purchase price, even assuming a reasonable worst-case scenario.

Note also that the market was not making very much of a distinction between the banks who likely had greater problems (BAC) and those who were much less affected (WFC). Wells Fargo did not require any TARP (Troubled Asset Relief Program) bailout money, and attempted, unsuccessfully, to refuse it. In fact, Wells Fargo's CEO, Dick Kovacevich, argued later that the TARP bailout was an "unmitigated disaster", stating that "TARP contributed to an unnecessary panic in the marketplace that still hasn't been fully restored."[41] His argument was that the government's forced distribution of bailout money to all of the banks, which was designed to attempt to restore confidence, actually had the opposite effect. At the time people did not know that even healthy banks were being forced to take TARP money against their will, hence causing many to believe that even healthy banks were in serious trouble. This caused the market to believe that the crisis was far greater than it was. In making this point, Kovacevich pointed to financial stocks plunging 80 percent within three months of the bank bailout as evidence that the TARP bailouts created a large amount of unnecessary fear in the marketplace.

The inefficient rationale here was that a combination of fear, verging on outright panic, coupled with loss aversion, problems with uncertainty, and a host of other minor contributing psychological forces were acting in concert to stampede the market herd into a selling frenzy, particularly with financial stocks. In addition, the fact that, unbeknownst to the market, otherwise sound financial institutions were forced to accept TARP money against their will likely created even greater fear and panic beyond that which was already irrationally present (although admittedly this was much clearer in hindsight than during the crisis). The rational investor who was able to think clearly along the lines of this variant perception and who was able to understand and postulate the underlying inefficient rationale was able to profit handsomely from this crisis. During times of such extreme fear and panic, the investors who can formulate a variant perception of reality and who can further understand the inefficient rationale as to why the market is behaving foolishly are likely the only ones who can make bold decisions during this time.

Thus to summarize the consensus view, the variant perception, and the inefficient rationale would have been as follows:

Consensus view: Large American banks are in serious financial trouble due to the subprime financial crisis, and they are at great risk of bankruptcy. In fact, the entire American economic system is at risk of failure. All of the banks are receiving bailout money, and hence all of them presumably need it. The future of the large banks is uncertain, and there is great potential for loss. Large capital raises may be required to guarantee solvency, diluting existing shareholders. Hence their stock prices should be severely discounted until this uncertainty is removed.

Variant perception: The American economy will recover. Although there are serious problems in the American financial system, current prices are reflective of a crisis of confidence that will pass. The large banks are very likely to survive this financial panic, and they will be worth far more than their current stock prices in a more normal environment. In addition, the large banks are selling at well below liquidation value, which provides ample margin of safety even in a worst-case scenario.

Inefficient Rationale: The market is experiencing a combination of loss aversion, uncertainty, and fear, which is causing the market to greatly

overreact to the crisis and thus behave irrationally. Further, market participants are engaged in short-term thinking, looking in the rearview mirror
as their sole guide to the future. This prevents them from envisioning the
banks operating in a more normal environment. Herd mentality coupled
with fear is causing outright panic in the market, causing people to sell
regardless of price. Thus the stocks of the large banks are priced not only
for failure, but also seemingly for complete economic collapse.

Bank of America stock (BAC) fell from its pre-crisis high of over $51
per share to a low of $3.59 per share in March 2009. The investor who
purchased BAC stock anywhere close to the low did extremely well, as
the stock price returned to over $16 per share less than 5 months later,
over a 4x increase in 5 months. Wells Fargo stock fell from its pre-crisis
high of over $34 to a low of $9.66 in March 2009. Two months later WFC
stock had almost tripled to around $27 per share.

4. Bank of America – 2011 Sovereign Debt Crisis

Let's further consider Bank of America stock during the "sovereign
debt crisis" of 2011. During late 2011 several European countries were
experiencing sovereign debt issues, most notably Greece, and to a lesser
extent Italy, Portugal and Spain. The sovereign debt crisis was headline
news for many weeks (the media loves a crisis – real or fabricated), and
there was considerable angst on the part of the general market. Many
market participants, after being shell-shocked only a few years earlier by
a very real financial crisis, were willing to believe the worst about this
new state of events. In fact, the general and financial media did a tremendous job of keeping the crisis front and center in everyone's mind
for a lengthy period of time, hence contributing to the general hysteria.

After the subprime financial crisis of 2008-9, BAC stock rebounded
from a low of $3 per share in March 2009 to a high of over $18 per share
in April 2010, only to fall back around 5$ per share during the height
of this new crisis. Bank of America actually had very little in the way of
sovereign debt exposure. Seemingly the dramatic fall in the stock price

was also at least partly due to a hangover from the first financial crisis, as well as concerns over its derivatives book and fears of a double-dip recession. At its low of just under $5 per share, BAC was trading at 40% of its tangible book value, which can be viewed as 40% of liquidation value. Thus if Bank of America had shut its doors and ran off its current business, it would be worth considerably more than its stock price. The consensus view, variant perception, and inefficient rationale for Bank of America would be roughly as follows:

Consensus view: Several European countries are at risk of sovereign debt default, creating great uncertainty. Further there is talk that some European countries, most notably Greece, will be asked or forced to leave the Euro. Large bank balance sheets are extremely opaque, and hence sovereign debt exposure is difficult to determine. The stock price of large banks and financial institutions should be severely discounted to reflect this uncertainty.

Variant perception: Bank of America seemingly has very little sovereign debt exposure, or at least less than the market currently believes. Bank of America's current problems are temporary in nature and will eventually go away. Bank of America has considerable earnings power, which will re-appear in a more normal environment. Plus, BAC stock is selling at well below liquidation value, which provides ample margin of safety even in a worst-case scenario. Further, the European Central Bank (ECB) has the power to address the current sovereign debt crisis – it merely needs to act.

Inefficient Rationale: The market is experiencing a combination of loss aversion, uncertainty, and fear, which is causing it to greatly over-react to the sovereign debt crisis and thus behave irrationally. Market participants see a potentially disruptive situation in Europe and are over-reacting to this negative uncertainty. Further, people are engaged in short-term thinking, looking in the rearview mirror as their sole guide to the future. This prevents people from envisioning a more normal environment. This tremendous fear and uncertainty has caused BofA to sell for much less than its liquidation value, which is an irrational pricing.

Bank of America stock (BAC) fell from its high of over $16 per share to a low of under $5 in December 2011. The investor who purchased BAC stock at any point in the fourth quarter of 2011 did well, as the stock price returned to over $16 per share approximately 2 years later, more than a 3x increase off of its low.

5. Disney – 2008 Financial Crisis

Before we leave the financial crises of 2009 and 2011, let's explore another tremendous bargain that was created by the Foolishness of the Crowd. (Note that virtually *every* stock was a bargain in March 2009, and many also were in 2011). Consider The Walt Disney Company (DIS). In September 2008, Disney stock traded at roughly $35 per share. Six months later, at the height of the financial crisis in March 2009, Disney traded at under $16 per share, less than book value. It seems almost crazy now to think that people would stop watching sports on ESPN, or stop watching Disney / Pixar movies, or that the company's theme parks would be deserted, as a result of the financial crisis. However, the company was essentially priced at liquidation value, almost as if it would never make money again. Disney stock rebounded to around $43 per share in early 2011, only to slide precipitously again to under $30 per share during the sovereign debt crisis of 2011. Again, it seems hard to believe that, because a few small European countries (notably Greece) were having debt repayment issues, that people would somehow stop viewing Disney content or attending Disney's parks. However, with a proper understanding of the necessary requirements for crowd wisdom, these mispricings become much easier to understand.

Here the consensus view, variant perception, and inefficient rationale would be as follows:

Consensus view: Economic Armageddon was very possibly at hand, either globally (2009) or in Europe (2011), and stocks should be heavily discounted in view of this uncertainty.

Variant perception: Disney was being offered for sale by the market at an absurdly low price in 2009 or at a bargain price in 2011. Further, Disney is a wide moat company with several valuable franchises, including ESPN, Disney movies and parks, and Pixar. Disney is worth considerably more than the current market price, and its value will be even greater in a more normal economic environment.

Inefficient Rationale: See immediately above, and substitute DIS for BAC or WFC.

As noted above, Disney stock (DIS) could have been purchased in March 2009 for under $16 per share and in September 2011 for under $30 per share. Fast-forward to mid 2014 and Disney is selling for well over $80 per share, a 5x increase from 2009 and close to a 3x increase from 2011. In addition, Disney is one of the few companies having a number of different strong "moats" – strong business franchises with little true competition, and hence pricing power. Examples of these moats include "Classic Disney" – the movies and characters from its extensive film library; Pixar, which is creating a whole new line of films and characters, theme parks – which complement and strengthen the film characters; ESPN – by far the dominant player in televised sports, and now Marvel (superheroes) and Lucasfilm (Star Wars and Raiders of the Lost Ark franchises). The chance to buy such a strong moat company at an extremely attractive price does not come along very often – the investor should bet big when the odds are heavily in his favor.

6. Berkshire Hathaway – Mispriced due to Indexation

A stock may become irrationally mispriced merely by being included or excluded from a certain index. Consider a situation where company A is part of a sector specific index, but generally does not share the characteristics of that index, or perhaps has much less of those characteristics than other companies in the index. In this situation, if the particular sector is predicted to do very well over the near term, many people will purchase the index, driving up the prices of all of the companies contained in the index. This will operate to drive up the price of company A along with every other company in the index, even though company A does not share the characteristics of the companies that form the basis of the optimism. Similarly, if the particular sector is predicted to do very poorly over the near term, many people will sell (or sell short) the index, driving down the prices of the companies contained in the index. This will operate to drive down the price of company A along with every other company in the index, even though company A does not share the characteristics of the companies that form the basis of the pessimism.

As an example of this phenomenon, consider during the sovereign debit "crisis" of 2011 when many people were shorting financial companies. During this period, Berkshire Hathaway stock underperformed the S&P 500 by over 10 percentage points, this occurring even though Berkshire is a member of the S&P 500 and has a large amount of capital invested in S&P 500 companies. A contributing factor, and perhaps the primary cause, of this underperformance was the fact that Berkshire Hathaway was the largest member of the S&P Financial Select Sector index, with a weighting of 9.12% in that index. This index contained companies such as Bank of America, JPMorgan Chase, Citigroup, AIG, and other financial companies, all predicted to perform extremely poorly in 2011. As a result, as of November 30, 2011 there were 247 million shares short of the Financial Select Sector SPDR ETF (XLF), which tracks this index. By the mere fact that Berkshire Hathaway was heavily weighted in this financial index, Berkshire had effectively become one of the most heavily shorted stocks in the United States.

However, Berkshire simply did not share the same characteristics as most of the financial companies in the Financial Select Sector Index. For example, as compared to these other financial institutions, Berkshire was much more conservatively capitalized, used little or no leverage, and had virtually no exposure to sovereign debt default. A simple valuation analysis at the time would have revealed that the market was considerably undervaluing Berkshire stock, i.e., Berkshire was being offered for sale in the market at much less than its intrinsic value. Simply because Berkshire was a heavily weighted member of this financial index, Berkshire's share price performance suffered along with other financial companies who were the actual targets of the short selling[42]. Even though Berkshire did not share the same characteristics as the other financial institutions in the index, it had been subject to the same massive sell-off merely due to its presence in the index. Berkshire stock was hence likely mispriced for at least this reason alone. This is a systemic inefficiency that would form the basis of an inefficient rationale – a rationale for the likely undervaluation of the respective stock.

Here the consensus view, variant perception, and inefficient rationale would be as follows:

Consensus view: Several European countries are at risk of sovereign debt default, creating great uncertainty. Further there is talk that some European countries, most notably Greece, will be asked, or forced, to leave the Euro. Stock prices in general should be severely discounted to reflect this uncertainty. Financial companies in particular will perform very poorly in the near term, and thus the Financial Select Sector Index should be sold or shorted.

Variant perception: Berkshire Hathaway is a very financially strong and secure company and has virtually no exposure to sovereign debt. Berkshire was actually a net provider of capital during the 2009 financial crisis. The company has very favorable near term and long-term prospects, and is underpriced at its current valuation. Berkshire's main businesses will largely be unaffected by this "crisis", e.g., people will not stop drinking Coke products or buying Geico insurance merely because Greece is experiencing debt problems.

Inefficient Rationale: The market is experiencing a combination of uncertainty, loss aversion, and fear, which is causing the market to greatly overreact to the sovereign debt crisis and thus behave irrationally. People are also engaged in short-term thinking, looking in the rearview mirror as their sole guide to the future and preventing them from envisioning a more normal environment. Further, Berkshire Hathaway is the largest component in a currently out of favor financial index. Since financial stocks are currently out of favor, this financial index is being heavily sold and sold short. As a result, the share price of Berkshire is being heavily discounted merely due to its presence in this index. However, Berkshire does not have the same characteristics as other financial companies in this index. This systemic inefficiency would be a cause for undervaluation in addition to the fear that was then pervading the overall market. Thus the drop in Berkshire's share price is largely due to indexation issues and overall fear, not fundamental issues.

In 2011 Berkshire Hathaway stock dropped from over $127,000 per A share to less than $100,00, and at its low was selling for almost book value. In fact, at a price/book close to 1, Berkshire was selling at its lowest valuation relative to book value in recent memory. Within a few years Berkshire A stock was trading at $190,000, a 90% increase.

Thus the development of both a variant perception and an inefficient rationale is a powerful combination, providing the investor with considerable confidence and resolve in going against the mainstream consensus, i.e., in making a large bet that goes against the herd. With any investment, a proper understanding of the consensus view is important, as the investor should understand the current thinking of the crowd, whatever merit it may have. In reaching a decision regarding a suitable investment, first the investor should develop some type of variant perception – some alternative viewpoint of the value of the company that differs from the consensus view. For a proposed investment to be a sound one according to value investing principles, there needs to be a significant discrepancy between the investor's valuation of the company and the price being offered by the market (the "margin of safety"). This discrepancy can only exist where the investor has some type of variant perception – a viewpoint on the valuation of the company that differs from the market view. Second, the investor should develop an inefficient rationale for the stock – a rationale as to why the market is presenting an incorrect price. Here the investor should carefully think through the reasons as to why the variant perception is allowed to exist in an otherwise mostly efficient market. As we have seen, the presence of both a strong variant perception and an inefficient rationale is a reliable predictor of a great investment. Social influence / cloning strategies, where applicable, may then form the third leg of this investment thesis.

There are a number of different types of inefficient rationales that can be developed, each being based on one or more identifiable crowd wisdom criteria that is lacking. For examples 3, 4 and 5 above the inefficient rationale was based on some type of macroeconomic event, such as a financial crisis. The inefficient rationale for examples 1 and 2 above was based on a crisis that only affected the respective individual company (a microeconomic crisis), e.g., the salad oil scandal for American Express and the Tylenol poisoning for Johnson & Johnson. The inefficient rationale for example 6 was largely based on the effects of indexation.

Short-term thinking can also serve as a basis for a good inefficient rationale and hence a good investment, especially when paired with a strong variant perception. Consider a company that encounters some temporary issues, and as a result has a one-time impairment to earnings. For example, this may be a company with good operating characteristics, but which has a subsidiary that is performing poorly and hence must be marked down in value, affecting one quarter's earnings. As another example, consider a company that operationally is performing well, but whose quarterly earnings are affected by one-time charges related to closing or remodeling some of its stores. Due to short-term thinking, the market often re-values the company based on these lower earnings, even though the problems that caused this decline in earnings is short-term in nature and non-recurring. This can especially be so if the market already has a negative viewpoint on the company, e.g., if the company is in an out-of-favor industry or one in a cyclical decline. If the investor becomes convinced that the lower earnings are truly non-recurring in nature, and hence is able to develop a strong variant perception regarding the value of the business, short-term thinking can serve as part or all of his inefficient rationale.

One of the reasons that an efficient rationale is a good predictor of stock mispricing is partly due to the wisdom of the crowd that is reflected in prices during more normal times when no inefficient rationale exists. For all of the discussion regarding the Foolishness of the Crowd, the market can be remarkably efficient in producing correct prices. When the various crowd wisdom criteria are largely present for a particular security, it is a fairly safe bet that, by means of crowd wisdom, the market is producing a somewhat correct price for the security. It can then be generally be assumed that if the crowd wisdom had previously been producing a certain price for a security, and some type of Foolishness of the Crowd event occurs and then fades away, leaving the company relatively intact and unchanged, over time the market will very likely return to its previous assessment of price.

For example, consider the first two case studies above. Prior to the negative events that occurred, i.e., the salad oil scandal and the Tylenol poisoning, the assumption was that, due to the wisdom of the crowd and the lack of any apparent inefficient rationale, the market was for the most part pricing these companies correctly. When the respective negative events occurred, the investor could rely on the Foolishness of the Crowd to produce a Foolish Offset from this previously correct price. Once the investor convinced himself that these events would in fact cause only a temporary impairment, and that the underlying business franchise was still sound, the investor could safely assume that this Foolishness would only last a short while. When the emotions had died down and the irrationality had faded away, the investor could rely on the market re-appraising the values of these companies at their previous levels.

The investor may also sometimes observe prior to a crisis that the market had in fact been overpricing certain stocks due to another form of irrationality. For example, prior to the financial crisis of 2008 the intelligent investor may have observed that the market was pricing the various financial companies too highly based on recent, large earnings from subprime mortgage lending that was clearly unsustainable. In this case, the investor may not be able to count on the market returning to these lofty valuations after the Foolishness of the Crowd wanes. Instead, however, the investor may be able to count on the notion that when a company with a high-flying stock encounters a serious crisis, the market's negative overreaction is usually quite severe. Thus in cases such as this the market is still likely to present a significant bargain.

Thus the premise in using the inefficient rational as a guide to investment is often that: 1) prior to the event(s) that caused the mispricing, the market very likely was ascribing the correct price to the stock, or perhaps may have been overpricing it due to other identifiable Foolishness; 2) when an event occurs that invokes the Foolishness of the Crowd, typically some aspect of uncertainty, loss aversion, fear and/or short-termism, the market will very likely overreact in a negative way, producing a negative Foolish Offset from the previous price, and hence presenting a bargain opportunity; and 3) once the overreaction fades away and the Foolishness of the Crowd has played out, the market will likely re-value the business to somewhere close to or above the previous price, i.e., the Foolish Offset will disappear.

Variant Perception and a Weak Inefficient Rationale

There will be times where the investor is able to form a variant perception, but there is a weak accompanying inefficient rationale. In other words, these are investments where the investor views the company through a different lens than the market consensus, i.e., the investor has developed an understanding of the future prospects of the company that are different than that of the market. However, except for possibly a weak form of short-term thinking, which is always present in the market to varying degrees, the investor is not able to point to any crowd psychology or behavioral missteps that would clearly indicate a stock mispricing. Thus here the investor primarily relies on the fact that he has identified long-term value in a company that the mostly rational, yet short-term minded, market has not. In this case, the investor essentially believes that he is smarter than the crowd with respect to this particular investment. As noted above, in this situation the investor must tread very carefully. A strong argument can be made that, for companies that are widely followed in the market, a stock mispricing (a variant perception) can generally only exist where there is an accompanying inefficient rationale. This is simply another way of stating that the wisdom of the crowd, being the powerful force that it is, will generally manifest in correct stock prices unless there is some underlying reason that produces an offset from this normal wisdom, i.e., unless one or more of the wisdom of the crowd criteria discussed in Chapter 3 is not present. Without some type of inefficient rationale, the investor is relying on his ability to outsmart the market – a dicey proposition.

Where a proposed investment has a strong variant perception but a very weak inefficient rationale, the investor should consider the nature of the company in terms of its size, following, and coverage by analysts. For a large, blue-chip stock that is widely followed by the market and is covered by a number of Wall Street analysts, absent some inefficient rationale the possibility that the investor sees value that the market does not is relatively low. For smaller stocks that are not widely followed, and perhaps are not covered by any analysts, and even better which are domiciled outside of the US, there is a much greater chance that the investor is able to discern value that the market does not.

Great investments have certainly been made when there has not been a very clear inefficient rationale, and where the investor to a large degree has simply been smarter than the market in identifying a bargain purchase. Warren Buffett's purchase of Coca Cola stock in the '80s would be an example of this. In the case of Buffett's Coca Cola purchase, there was no market panic or other psychological explanation for undervaluation, the "New Coke" debacle had played itself out three years earlier, and there were also no systemic market inefficiency issues that one could point to for undervaluation. Rather, Buffett saw a company with a very strong brand and immense international expansion capabilities, coupled with a change in leadership that produced a re-newed focus on its core products. The inefficient rationale would have been short-term thinking – the market's myopic focus on current and near-term earnings which blinded it to potentially large international earnings growth. In large part, however, in making his purchase of Coca Cola stock, Buffett was simply smarter than the crowd. Much the same can be said of Buffett's earlier purchase of Disney stock in 1965. Buffett realized that the business franchise, and in particular Disney's film li-brary, were being seriously undervalued by the market. The inefficient rationale would again have been short-term thinking, in particular the market's tendency to only value, or at least significantly overweight, current earnings, and to ignore assets with latent earning power. Here again though, in large part Buffett was simply smarter than the market in identifying a bargain.

However, with the introduction of the Internet, online stock screen-ing tools, investor blogs, and overall improved financial reporting, bar-gains in the stock market that are not clearly based on some identifiable market inefficiency, while still present, are harder to come by than they perhaps used to be. Further, very few of us have the business and in-vesting acumen of Warren Buffett to identify these great investments without some form of market irrationality pointing the way, and in fact many of Buffett's best investments occurred during periods of great fear in the market. One of the central theses of this book is that the predict-ability and reliability of crowd irrationality is in most instances a better predictor of an outstanding investment than any individual investor's valuation analysis. In short, the wisdom (or in this case Foolishness) of the crowd is much stronger than the wisdom of any single individual.

9. FINDING BARGAINS IN A MACROECONOMIC CRISIS

The concept of an inefficient rationale, the investor's newfound knowledge of the Foolishness of the Crowd, will be a tremendous aid in investment decisions during times of extreme macroeconomic situations. In order to better understand the ways in which an investor can use this concept, let's explore the different macroeconomic scenarios that he will encounter. Here it is not only important that the investor be able to recognize that the Foolishness of the Crowd is likely present, but also to understand the various factors at play in producing this Foolishness. Evaluation of the Foolishness of the Crowd in a macroeconomic scenario typically occurs when either: a) some type of macroeconomic "crisis" is currently underway, or some market correction has occurred, causing much fear and uncertainty among participants in the market; or b) some form of unbridled optimism or happiness is present in the market, and people think that things can only get better. The subjective (qualitative) factors that should be considered in assessing the Foolishness of the Crowd will necessarily depend on which form of Foolishness currently prevails. Let's first consider a stock downturn caused by a macroeconomic crisis.

Macroeconomic crises are easily visible once they take form. However, spotting them before they come to fruition can be incredibly difficult. Consider the financial crisis of 2008-09 and the sovereign debt crisis of 2011. Some were able to discern ahead of time that a large amount of subprime mortgage lending, which involved lending to uncreditworthy borrowers, often with terms that included rising interest rates, was bound to end badly. Very few were able to predict this crisis with enough conviction to actually take economic advantage of it. Similarly, very few were able to assess ahead of time that sovereign debt in some European countries was a major issue that could be financially exploited. On the whole, the causative factors that produce many types of macroeconomic crises are difficult to identify prior to the crisis (although after the crisis, due to hindsight bias and outright hubris, a number of pundits will inevitably talk about how "they saw it coming," even though they gave no hint of this foresight before the crisis). Despite the above, market participants are heartily encouraged to pay attention to the macroeconomic picture, and to remain especially wary and vigilant when things get frothy and easy money is being made. Knowledge of behavioral psychology can certainly assist the investor in interpreting macroeconomic events, and may help keep the investor out of trouble the next time credit, leverage, and/or exuberance get out of hand. A stock market crisis, e.g., the bursting of a market bubble, may be somewhat easier to predict, as crowd irrationality will be very much on display. However, although knowledge of market psychology will be very useful during such times, estimating the degree of irrationality and hence the timing of such an event is still quite difficult.

When a macroeconomic crisis occurs or a market bubble bursts, there will be great fear and panic in the marketplace, especially as depicted in the media. There will be a continual drumbeat of bad news, accompanied by massive selling of stocks that will drive down prices to bargain levels. The fear of loss will be paramount in people's minds, and it will be hard to not follow the herd. During such times it is hugely important for the investor to have the ability to: 1) stay detached from this panic; 2) realize that an overreaction to the crisis is almost assuredly taking place; 3) realize that many stocks will hence be oversold and at bargain prices; and 4) take action and submit buy orders during this period.

Sir John Templeton was a renowned value investor and perhaps his most famous quote is: "The time of maximum pessimism is the best time to buy, and the time of maximum optimism is the best time to sell." However, even Templeton realized the difficulty in purchasing stocks at times of fear and panic. In recognizing this difficulty, during normal economic times when the markets were calm, Templeton would make a list of companies that he would like to buy if they were selling at a more attractive price. He would then place buy limit orders on these selected stocks at extremely low prices, i.e., at prices well below current market values, counting on these buy orders to be automatically filled at these low limit prices during a panic. In the event of a sharp sell off during a market panic, the limit orders would be executed, and Templeton would purchase shares in the companies he desired at very good prices.

Thus Templeton automated a way to purchase securities at bargain prices during a panic, in large part because he knew the pain and anguish he would feel in going against the herd and buying stocks during the actual panic. Templeton understood that humans are innately herd animals, and when those around us are consumed with fear and panic, we tend to panic as well. During times of market fear and panic, investors lose the capability of independent, rational judgment and tend to freeze in fear at the exact moment when they should be buying aggressively. Templeton's strategy was designed to take his own human frailty and emotions out of the equation. If such a great value investor as Sir John Templeton required assistance in making the right decisions during a market crisis, it would seem that less skilled and experienced investors will at least need similar help and encouragement. Therefore it is very important that the investor ensure that he maintains his rationality during a crisis, i.e., that he makes sure he keeps his head while everyone else is losing theirs.

Fortunately there are a number of things an investor can do to help ensure his rationality during a crisis. First and foremost, the investor needs to arm himself with the knowledge to act boldly, specifically in the areas of valuation and psychology. Having done so, the investor will then be in a position to take certain actions during the crisis to help ensure rationality. As discussed above, when the investor is making a seemingly bargain purchase during a time of rapid market decline, it is absolutely critical that he make a dispassionate, rational estimation of the intrinsic value of the companies in which he is considering investing.

If the investor convinces himself that his estimation of the intrinsic value of a company is far greater than the current stock market price, and if there is little or no chance of serious impairment of that value as a result of the crisis, then the investor must have the fortitude to act. During the crisis, the investor should obviously periodically review any prior analysis he has made and make sure that significant facts or assumptions that he has relied upon have not changed.

However, as discussed above, for many investors reliance solely on valuation principles and estimates of intrinsic value (the investor's variant perception) will simply not be sufficient. When the stock market is declining rapidly and fear and panic are widely prevalent, there is great temptation from both an intellectual and psychological standpoint to believe that the crowd may be right. At best, the investor will inevitably begin to doubt his valuations, and even a small amount of doubt can lead to inaction, or even worse, incorrect action, especially when a number of psychological forces are acting in concert telling you to sell rather than buy. Thus some additional confidence is needed to help ensure he is capable of making the right decisions during a market panic.

As noted above, one of the most important and helpful things to an investor during a market panic is to develop an "inefficient rationale" – the knowledge, and more particularly the thesis or rationale, as to exactly *why* the market is behaving as it is, i.e., why companies are being offered for sale at absurdly low prices. If the investor does not have a good rationale as to why the crowd is collectively offering low, even foolish, prices, he is more likely to presume that the crowd is right and he is wrong, and he is unlikely to have sufficient confidence to go against the crowd.

Thus here we discuss in greater detail the main reasons for market overreaction during a panic. The investor will be in a much better position to form his inefficient rationale if he can actively identify the factors prevailing in the marketplace contributing to market irrationality. In other words, the investor will be in a much better position to form a rationale of market irrationality if he is on the lookout for and is capable of recognizing the factors contributing to the Foolishness of the Crowd. Further, and perhaps more importantly, the investor will have much greater confidence in his inefficient rationale to the extent he recognizes the causative reasons for irrationality in the marketplace. Such confidence may make the difference in the investor being able to act upon the opportunities presented for financial gain.

There are a number of different forms of irrationality that come into play in a crisis and operate to drive down stock prices. First and foremost are the psychological factors of loss aversion, fear, recency bias and herd mentality, which act together in a lollapalooza effect to cause mass selling of stocks regardless of valuation. Loss aversion causes people to literally run away from situations that present the risk of loss. Fear works hand in hand with loss aversion, as participants not only greatly desire to avoid a loss scenario, but in addition are very likely actively watching their own portfolio values drop precipitously on an almost daily basis. The experience of these actual losses, coupled with our natural tendency toward loss aversion, incites fear and panic and a huge desire to sell everything to simply avoid the possibility (and pain) of further loss. The astute investor will easily observe this panicked selling in the marketplace, as market participants race for the exits. The investor will also observe news reports in the popular press describing fear in the market as well as mass selling by participants to avoid further losses.

Recency bias causes people to extrapolate the current economic and market climate out well into the future, and hence believe that the current negative conditions are here to stay, and that things will "never get better." Here the investor will see news reports touting the current negative state of the economy and the market as a permanent condition. Given the short-term mindset of most market participants, anything lasting more than 6 months will likely be viewed as substantially permanent. Finally, herd mentality is a very powerful amplifying force. As participants see the stock price declines in the market, indicating that everyone else is selling too, and given that virtually every form of television, radio and print media is yelling SELL, the tendency for everyone to follow the herd is extremely strong. Here the investor will have observed a marked increase in the number of sell orders, or an increase in the ratio of buy orders to sell orders. More generally, the investor will see news reports of mass and indiscriminate selling, without regard to value. Further, as described previously, the principal object of media companies is to earn advertising profits by attracting as much viewership as possible, not to provide objective news reporting. Media company advertising is closely tied to customer viewership or audience market share ratings. Thus the various news media sources are incentivized to exaggerate and hype virtually any situation, portraying minor events as crises to attempt to increase its number of viewers.

A host of other lesser psychological biases will also be at play here, including anchoring (as people use the new price lows as anchor points in their thinking), confirmation bias (as people seek out evidence to confirm their worst fears and ignore evidence that things may not be as bad as they seem), overconfidence bias (as people are sufficiently overconfident of their own abilities to resist questioning their beliefs), and perhaps many more. Although these psychological phenomena are not readily apparent to the casual observer, the investor can be certain as to their presence and influence in the market. Remember that perhaps the one constant in our ever-changing world is human nature. The investor can be assured that the psychology of misjudgment will be playing itself out in each participant's mind, collectively producing predictable pricing errors in the overall market.

A secondary factor contributing to a selloff during a panic is the short-term mindset of most market participants, including Wall Street money managers and analysts. Due to their focus on next quarter's results, most Wall Street analysts make their buy and sell recommendations based on how they believe a particular company will do *next quarter*. However the economic conditions during a crisis or panic are decidedly abnormal, and thus the normal short-term financial metrics for a company will be decidedly negative. For example, next quarter's earnings estimates are bound to be low. Also consider the added factor of recency bias, mentioned above, falsely suggesting that current conditions will persist longer than they actually will, which provides people with a convenient rationalization as to why basing their valuation estimates on current conditions is appropriate. Accordingly, many market participants, with their focus on quarterly results and their incorrect belief that this is "the new normal," will incorrectly price assets based solely on current conditions, whereas a more intelligent and rational appraisal of the intrinsic value of the business would be based on how the company would fare in a more normal climate, and with a long-term horizon in mind. The investor will observe analyst reports and media commentary espousing negative views on various companies, primarily based on their near term earnings outlook. Most of the Wall Street analysis will be sell recommendations based on what the analysts predict for next quarter's earnings.

A third factor contributing to a selloff is not related to either poor fundamental assessment of a company or psychology. This factor relates to the particular characteristics of a marketplace. In particular, when a large selloff occurs, participants who are leveraged are likely to receive margin calls and are thus forced to sell, adding further selling pressure to already depressed stock prices. The investor should be on the alert for reports of margin calls and other forms of distressed selling.

The primary way the Foolishness of the Crowd can be exploited in a crisis is first by the simple realization that after such a crisis begins the Foolishness of the Crowd will almost certainly be present to a large degree. The investor should further be aware of these forces and their causative factors, and he should actively seek out confirming evidence that these factors are present. The investor will thus be in a better position to form a contrarian thesis, a variant perception, that is different from the consensus view. The investor should also develop an "inefficient rationale" as described above, which is a rationale as to why the market is incorrect, i.e., why the so-called wisdom of the market crowd is not producing the correct stock price. Having done so, as prices fall greatly below intrinsic value, the investor will recognize this as the time to buy. His variant perception and inefficient rationale will provide comfort and assurance as to the opportunities being presented, and he will be much less likely to second guess himself and fall victim to the paralyzing fear of the herd.

At first blush, in light of our previous discussion, and perhaps considered from the comfort of one's armchair during somewhat normal economic times and market moods, this may seem an almost trivial realization. However, in the heat of the moment, when panic and fear are swirling around, knowledge and awareness as to *why* the events are unfolding as they are is a huge advantage. The knowledge that the market panic and resulting bargain prices are due to psychological biases and irrationality (Foolishness), and not underlying changes in valuation, provides a serious benefit to the investor, providing him with the assurance to calmly step forth and buy stocks at bargain basement prices when everyone else is selling.

As previously discussed, turning social influence to your advantage is one of the most powerful ways to stay detached from the influence of the irrational crowd. Nowhere is this more important than during times of fear and panic. During a macroeconomic crisis, the investor should seek out the company and conversation of like-minded value investors. A key recommendation is for the investor to join an online value investing forum and read, and actively participate in, the commentary from other value investors. During a macroeconomic crisis and a resulting large market decline, the investor will be able to read intelligent commentary from others about the foolishness of the market, and even more importantly will be able to correspond and interact with others who are actively buying securities. Such forums can be a huge support network for the investor, providing constant reminder that the investor is not the "only one" who is going against the mainstream. Further, as discussed above, the investor should attempt to "tune out" as much of the conventional crowd noise as possible, e.g., by limiting his exposure to the various commentators on financial television channels. The media is incentivized to overdo and over-dramatize any significant event, portraying every somewhat significant negative macro event as a crisis. Thus the investor should view conventional financial news with a heavy dose of skepticism, and he should attempt to glean factual developments from conventional financial news while not getting caught up in the hysteria.

The investor should also closely follow the actions and commentary of the great value investors during this time. During a lengthy market decline the investor is able to track and compare what the great investors have bought. In addition, many of the great investors will often appear on television and in interviews trumpeting their recent stock purchases and explaining the rationales and theories on certain investments. Following great investors who are buying during a downturn, instead of listening to the conventional wisdom of the crowd, is time well spent. In particular, during a time of market distress, if a particular sector (e.g., financials) is being affected by the crisis, the investor may be able to seek out value-based fund managers who have expertise in that sector.

From my own experience, during the sovereign debt "crisis" of 2011 I realized that a number of the banks and other financial institutions were being unfairly penalized, due in part to a hangover from the 2009 financial crisis, the incorrect perception of their exposure to sovereign debt issues, and in large part due to the overdone mania on the part of mainstream market participants. During this time I was fortunate to have placed approximately 85% of my stock portfolio in just 3 stocks (common stocks and TARP warrants), these being Berkshire Hathaway, AIG, and Bank of America. This was a rare opportunity to buy Berkshire Hathaway, Warren Buffett's company, at book value, and I considered this the absolute safest of long-term investments. Purchasing large stakes in AIG and BofA required considerably more courage and fortitude. I had selected these two as being the most hated of the financial companies, and hence the most likely undervalued by the market. They were the poster children of the financial crisis, requiring considerable government bailouts to ensure their survival. One of the main things that stiffened my backbone during this time was an interview given by

Bruce Berkowitz of the Fairholme Funds[43], where he explained his thesis on Bank of America and AIG. Every so often, with the rampant, widespread pessimism all about me, when doubt would begin to creep into my mind, I would go back and replay the interview and listen again to his presentation of the investment thesis. Here I was struck by both the merits of his arguments both from a valuation perspective and a psychological perspective, as well as the confidence he displayed despite his positions initially being underwater. These interviews enabled me to have the courage to not only buy initial stakes in these companies, but to increase my stakes whenever I had the opportunity to do so.

Another difficulty is that a person buying bargain stocks during a time of crisis will very rarely (seemingly almost never) buy at the exact bottom. Usually the investor will have bought in the midst of a decline in price of the particular stock, and hence the stock will continue to decline after the investor's purchase. For example, assume the investor estimates the intrinsic value of a company to be $70 per share, and during a crisis he has the opportunity to buy the stock at $45 per share. After this seemingly bargain purchase the stock price declines further to $30 per share, and the investor is now showing large paper losses on his purchase. This may cause even the most courageous of investors to begin to doubt their decision. Here the investor can do several things to maintain his courage. First, he can revisit his variant perception by double-checking his facts, his estimates of the intrinsic value of the business, which may be based on a number of metrics, such as the company's earning power in a more normal environment. Second, he should revisit his inefficient rationale – continually reminding himself of the psychology at play in the market, the irrationality that is occurring. Perhaps the investor should watch some of the more extreme financial news shows to reassure himself that he wants no part of the irrationality of the mainstream crowd. Beyond assessing and rechecking intrinsic value estimates, and reminding himself of the irrationality involved, the investor can take the additional steps outlined above, namely maintaining considerable contact with his various value investing support groups such as friends, Internet boards, and following the great value investors. Here the investor must demonstrate considerable resolve in not beginning to second guess himself and begin thinking that perhaps the crowd is right. Virtually everything the investor will see and hear during this time, from the market, news commentators, market pundits, brokers, etc. will be "sell." The above steps are the best defense the investor can take to help ensure that he is not taken in by the Foolishness of the Crowd.

Considering the above, a question that arises is how the investor can determine the best time to buy a stock during a downturn. A related question involves whether the investor should make a number of small purchases during the market decline, or attempt to wait for an identifiable bottom before beginning his purchases. In "The Intelligent Investor", Benjamin Graham discussed the possibility of the intelligent investor being able to profit from the "pendulum swings" or wide fluctuations in common stock prices. Here Graham made a distinction between attempting to do this by "way of *timing*" and by "way of *pricing*", which he explained as follows:

> By timing we mean the endeavor to anticipate the action of the stock market – to buy or hold when the future course is deemed to be upward, to sell or refrain from buying when the course is downward. By pricing we mean the endeavor to buy stocks when they are quoted below their fair value and to sell them when they rise above such value.[44]

Graham advised that an attempt to precisely "time" the bottom of a market downturn based solely on macroeconomic forecasting will prove largely ineffective. Attempts to predict future market movements in and of themselves are generally completely unreliable, and add credence to the notion that trying to time the bottom of the market is largely a fool's game. In contrast, using pricing in determining appropriate buy and sell decision points is a very effective strategy, as we have discussed. In other words, the investor should have some estimate of the intrinsic values of businesses that he is considering for investment, and when stock prices fall during a downturn to a level well below the investor's estimate of intrinsic value, then that is the time to buy. Therefore, the relative difference between the current market price and an estimate of the intrinsic value of the underlying business (the "margin of safety") is the best guide for determining when to make a stock purchase.

Now consider whether the Foolishness of the Crowd can be used as an aid to determine the best *time* to buy a stock during a downturn. We believe that it can, at least to a limited degree. In particular, the investor may be able to at least approximately assess the degree of a market downturn based on the level of fear and panic in the market, i.e., the investor may be able to better assess the "time of maximum pessimism" by gauging the crowd's sentiment. Here a study of the history of past stock downturns and their causative economic events may be extremely useful, as they can be used to form a rough gauge or benchmark to which one can compare current events. The investor can then make a rough estimate of the seriousness of the current crisis, as well as the amount of fear and panic in the marketplace as represented in the financial media. He can then compare current events with his studied history of previous crises and the approximate amount of stock undervaluation that occurred during these prior downturns. The simple proposition is that a more serious economic crisis is bound to lead to more fear and panic in the marketplace and hence to a greater drop in stock prices, whereas a less serious macroeconomic situation will produce less fear and panic and hence a somewhat lesser decrease in stock prices. This assessment is necessarily qualitative in nature and far from foolproof. Certainly, discrepancy between price and value as taught by Graham is the most reliable guide as to when to make stock transactions. However, a qualitative estimate of the degree of the Foolishness of the Crowd can also be of some assistance in this decision.

Another way that can be used to gauge the best time to buy a particular stock during a crisis is ironically to use the wisdom of the crowd effect from a select pool of market participants as a guide. The crowd being referred to here is the relatively small community of value investors. Here we posit the fundamental assertion that, whereas the larger speculative crowd can at times be a "foolish" crowd, the relatively small value investing crowd is very often a "wise" crowd (or "wiser" crowd) during these same times. We believe that the value investing crowd is a "wise" crowd based on the belief that this crowd 1) is much more independent and hence less subject to herd mentality than the larger speculative crowd; 2) applies a better overall thought and decision-making process to their investment decisions; and 3) is much more rational than the average market participant. It is acknowledged that the above statements are more opinion than proven fact, but they are likely provable to some degree in the sense that the investment records of the value investing crowd are generally superior to the crowd as a whole.

During some point in large stock downturn, a number of different value investors will begin taking similar positions in undervalued stocks. The various times in which these investors began initiating positions can act as a rough guide to the time at which the wisdom of this crowd recognizes a value proposition. In addition, the fact that a number of other value investors, with whom the investor will likely have some familiarity through mutual participation in an online forum, are taking positions will provide comfort and resolve to the investor. Thus not only is the investor taking advantage of a true wisdom of the crowd effect, he is also using social influence to his advantage.

Following and cloning the investment decisions of well-respected value investors can be particularly effective during a serious downturn because many of the great value investors are often "early" in purchasing bargain securities during times of great fear and panic. Accomplished value investors are well versed in identifying value situations, and at some point during a downturn one or more stocks will become significantly undervalued. Value investors will recognize this large discrepancy between price and value and will begin purchasing stock. However, predicting the bottom of the stock, which is tantamount to predicting the degree of irrationality of the crowd, is very difficult, and is generally not attempted by most. In other words, very few, if any, value investors spend time and effort attempting to assess the degree of irrationality present in the market. Thus accomplished value investors will begin purchasing when a value proposition (margin of safety) exists, and in times of greater economic distress will tend to underestimate the irrationality at play in the market. After the value investors begin establishing a position in a value stock, during times of serious economic distress the stock prices will inevitably keep going lower, possibly much lower.

Therefore, during a severe crisis, many of the great value investors will inevitably be early in their purchase decisions. In general, the greater the severity of the macroeconomic crisis, the greater the amount of fear and panic, and the more likely it is that the great value investors will be "early" in their value-based stock purchases. Whereas precisely estimating the bottom of the market in a market downturn is extremely difficult, a qualitative estimation of the degree of irrationality present in the market can provide at least some assistance as to when to stage one's buying during a downturn. Thus perhaps an ideal strategy in a serious macroeconomic crisis is to follow or copy the investment decisions of the great value investors (supported by your own independent analysis of course), but to lag these investment decisions by a period of time, wherein this period of time lag is based on a qualitative assessment of the degree of Foolishness in the market. In other words, the investor may want to "tune" the amount of lag in following other value investors based on the perceived severity of the economic crisis – the greater the severity, the larger the amount of lag.

During a stock downturn caused by relatively moderate economic distress, the investor should likely initiate a position in an undervalued stock relatively quickly after 1) identifying a sufficient margin of safety in the undervalued stock based on his own intrinsic value estimation; and also 2) learning of (or seeing confirmation in) the opportunity from one or more well regarded value investors. However, during a stock downturn caused by relatively severe economic distress, the investor would be advised to wait some period of time to initiate a position after the value investing crowd jumps in, or perhaps to more slowly stage acquiring his position than he otherwise would have. Here he is counting on the tendency of the value investing crowd to begin purchasing a stock when a value proposition exists, and without considering the degree of irrationality, and hence the degree of margin of safety, that will eventually manifest in the stock price. However, it is noted that there is some danger in waiting to purchase stocks during a severe downturn until after a "clear" bottom in stock prices. First of all, there will be no "clear" bottom in the market, as the market will inevitably rise and fall numerous times during a downturn, and perceived bottoms will often only be temporary in nature. However, an even greater danger in waiting to purchasing stocks during the following upturn is that the investor may be less inclined psychologically to make purchases at a more expensive price than he could have gotten only days or weeks earlier. In other words, once stock prices begin moving upward in a more regular fashion, the investor will be in a position of knowing that "he coulda got it cheaper" and may be less inclined to invest. The investor needs to strike a delicate balance between patience and inaction.

To summarize our advice for investing during a stock market decline, the investor should rely on: 1) his variant perception – his own estimates of intrinsic value of the businesses in which he is considering investing, which will be different than the market consensus; 2) an inefficient rationale predicated on the Foolishness of the Crowd, including as well a viewpoint based on the predictability of this Foolishness – knowing that the amount of Foolishness will increase with the amount of fear or depression in the market; and 3) the wisdom of the value investing crowd in identifying undervalued securities, albeit with some time offset applied, wherein the amount of crowd irrationality (Foolishness) is used to gauge this amount of time offset.

Thus the investor is advised to perform a rigorous analysis of the companies in which he is considering investing, understand the degree of psychological foolishness that is occurring in the marketplace, and keep track of the actions of other respected value investors. In the best of all worlds, the investor comes up with an estimate of intrinsic value that is well below the current market price, he is able to gauge the degree of market mania, and hence the likely degree of foolish mispricing, as extremely high, and other value investors have recently taken large positions. The above circumstances do not occur very often in an investor's lifetime, and in this case he should recall the old adage that one should "bet big when the odds are heavily in your favor."

There may be times when the investor may correctly perceive that fear is rampant in the market, and that in particular a large degree of pessimism is heaped on a particular company, but his valuation estimates do not indicate that the respective company is undervalued. Depending on the financial acumen of the investor, his inefficient rationale may be a better indication of value than his variant perception, i.e., the Foolishness of the Crowd may well likely be more indicative of mispricing than the investor's quantitative estimates of value. In other words, the presence of collective irrationality during certain conditions, the collective Foolishness, may likely be a more accurate indication of a good investment than a single person's analytical valuation result. Here we do not recommend that the investor act against his analytical reasoning. Rather, the above circumstances should cause the investor should go back recheck his analysis and assumptions.

As an example of this from my own experience, when I first analyzed the financial statements of AIG in 2011, I was not able to convince myself that AIG was significantly undervalued, despite the intense market hatred of the company and the huge decline in stock price.

Fortunately, my faith that the Foolishness of the Crowd was virtually certain to produce mispricing caused me to go back and recheck my analysis. Upon further thought, I realized that I was valuing AIG by solely considering its financial performance based on current unfavorable circumstances and during the current distressed economic climate, which were both fairly certain to pass. A much more intelligent analysis would estimate the value of AIG based on its likely earning power in a more normal environment. This more informed intrinsic value estimate provided the impetus to take a fairly large position in AIG at a very attractive price. Another important factor in my decision process during this time was the investment thesis on AIG espoused by several notable value investors, which significantly increased my confidence during this time period. Thus, during times of market distress the investor should make investments with the confidence that comes from conservative estimates of intrinsic value being well above the market price (a large margin of safety); knowing the market's irrationality will be reflected in stock prices; and guidance from a wise crowd of fellow value investors.

Opportunities in a Macroeconomic Crisis

In most any major crisis the overall stock market is likely to decline to some extent, and to some degree the selling will be indiscriminate, as people sell their stakes in mutual funds, index funds, and ETFs to simply escape the market. As examples of this, during the financial crisis of 2008-9 the stock market went in a freefell, and during the sovereign debt crisis of 2011 a number of companies were selling at values that promised a large margin of safety. Several examples of these were provided in Chapter 8. Thus in a market panic it is likely that a number of great companies will be selling at fire sale prices. Here the investor would be best equipped if he had a list of good companies which meet his criteria for investment, except for price, so that when the crisis and the resulting stock market decline occurs he will be poised to act and act decisively to the bargains presented.

Another way to better exploit the Foolishness of the Crowd during a crisis is to gain an understanding of which sectors and/or which specific companies are most affected by the crisis. In other words, in which companies is the fear the greatest? In a macroeconomic crisis, there are likely to be a certain sector and/or specific companies that are the focal point of the crisis, and these are where the best opportunities will be. Consider the financial crisis of 2008-9, where the financial sector was the obvious source of the crisis. During this time the greatest movement in the herd was out of financial stocks, and hence the best bargains lay in the financial sector. Therefore, in at least some types of crisis there will be companies or entire sectors that are the focal point of the crisis, and these companies are ideal candidates for possible investment. The investor can apply the principles discussed above by forming a variant perception, an inefficient rationale, and using social influence to his advantage. In addition, as we discussed above, the investor must be able to convince himself that the company will survive. If the survival of the company is in doubt, then the investor must convince himself that the price of the company is far less than liquidation value and there is a small likelihood management will fritter away these assets trying to turn around a dying business

Microeconomic Crises

Much of the above discussion with respect to macroeconomic crises also applies to microeconomic crises which only affect individual companies. For example, consider the above example of American Express and its "salad oil scandal." Here the stock price dropped from $60 to a low of $35, based largely on fears that were unfounded, and as Buffett demonstrated with some amount of research were provable at the time to be unfounded. Consider also the case of British Petroleum (BP) after the gulf oil spill in 2010, after which the stock dropped from $60 per share to about $27 per share. Again the crowd, in part driven by the negative hysteria in the media, overreacted to the bad news, and stock returned close to $50 per share in a little over 6 months. In the BP oil spill situation, the stock prices of a number of offshore drilling companies were also affected, and these would also have been great investments as well. Consider also the case of Johnson & Johnson after the Tylenol poisonings in 1982. After news reports that several people had died from consuming Tylenol laced with poison, the market value of Johnson & Johnson's stock price declined by almost 30%. Interestingly, a number of other firms in the industry also suffered marked share price declines as a fallout over the uncertainty of new packaging regulations and their effect on the industry. In each of these situations the stock price of the respective company collapsed immediately following the crisis, only to largely return to close to their prior share price some months later.

As discussed earlier, when considering purchase of stock in a company that is currently undergoing some type of crisis and which is hence out of favor, it is critical that the investor confirm to the best of his ability that the underlying business franchise of the company is intact. In other words, the investor must confirm that the problems being encountered by the compare are both short-term and solvable. If the problems are endemic to the overall business of the company (think buggy whip makers around the turn of the century or typewriter companies in the 1980's), then the company is not suitable for investment. However, if the underlying business of the company is sound, then after thorough analysis the investor will readily be able to convince himself that the company will survive the current crisis and return to some semblance of its former strength.

10. AVOIDING DISASTER IN A STOCK MARKET BUBBLE

In considering the scenario of unbridled optimism, where stock prices advance well beyond their intrinsic values, knowledge of valuation principles and the Foolishness of the Crowd will be of great benefit. The two defenses of: 1) knowledge of valuation principles and 2) knowledge of market psychology enable the investor to avoid falling into the trap of participating in a market bubble. The investor's knowledge of valuation principles allows him to stay firmly rooted in the facts of intrinsic value, thus helping to insulate him from the emotions of the greedy crowd. The investor's knowledge of market psychology will primarily be in recognizing that the Foolishness of the Crowd is in large part the cause of the observed overvaluation. Let's discuss each of these in turn.

The intelligent investor will (or should) have some estimate of the intrinsic values of the businesses in which he is invested. As the stock price approaches these estimated intrinsic values, the intelligent investor should consider selling his positions, especially if there are much better bargains available. Once the stock price gets reasonably close to intrinsic value, the investor no longer has a margin of safety in his investment. Thus his potential for future returns is no longer based on a large discrepancy between price and value, and the market's tendency to correct such discrepancies over the long term. Rather, his potential for future returns necessarily lies in the hope that the market will price the business at higher than its intrinsic value. This is a form of the "greater fool" theory, which is the belief that the investor will be able to sell the stock at a price higher than intrinsic value to a greater fool. While certainly there is no question that greater fools are out there, depending on such a greater fool for a profit is simply too unreliable to be used as a basis for continued investment. Certainly the purchase of a stock at or above its intrinsic value is in the realm of speculation, not investment. Similarly, holding on to an existing stock with knowledge that the price has risen to or above its intrinsic value may also be considered as within the realm of speculation, one exception for this being the desire to hold on to great businesses which promise to continue compounding their book values at high rates of return.

Thus when the price of a stock begins approaching or reaches intrinsic value, the investor should likely begin, or at least consider, selling his position. During a period of optimism, such as during a bubble, the stock price may continue to rise above intrinsic value. The investor will likely have begun liquidating his position by the time the stock price reaches intrinsic value, but yet the stock price may continue to rise. Here the investor must be extremely careful, as there is a great temptation for him to think, "perhaps I have misappraised the business in some way; perhaps the company is really worth a lot more than what I thought; perhaps the market is right." The investor is watching the stock price rise, knowing that he is missing out on "easy profits." He had initially made a correct call on purchase of the stock, based on his initial estimate of its intrinsic value being well below the then stock price, and had the courage to purchase the stock when it was out of favor. Now, although he has been selling, or has sold out, his position and has made a profit on the stock, the stock price is advancing further. The investor gets the distinct feeling that he is missing out on the party. There is great temptation for him to "jump back into" the stock, to repurchase it.

None other than Sir Isaac Newton, perhaps one of the greatest minds ever, fell into this trap. Newton had purchased shares in the South Sea Trading Company and later sold those shares for a profit. However, the stock continued to rise after he sold. The hype and the mania continued, and Newton could not resist the temptation to jump back into the stock at a higher price. After Newton had re-established his position, the bubble burst, and Newton ended up losing most of his personal wealth. After this experience, Newton is reputed to have famously commented:

"I can calculate the movement of the stars, but not the madness of men".[44] In terms of stock market bubbles, the South Sea Bubble is an exceptional case because it was rife with bribery, self-dealing, and out-right fraud. Regardless, if one of the most intelligent men who ever lived can fall into the trap of a stock market bubble, we mortals must remain extra vigilant.

During a period of market euphoria, or irrational exuberance, when stock prices are generally rising above their intrinsic values, how best can the investor stay grounded in reality and resist the temptation to join the party? The investor's first defense is to maintain his estimates of intrinsic value firmly in mind, and have decided ahead of time that he will not purchase a security at or above his estimate regardless of the circumstance. It will be admittedly difficult to not join in the pursuit of supposedly easy money. As the investor is continually bombarded with stories of how the masses are "getting rich in the stock market", the investor must maintain his discipline and not purchase overpriced securities. Further, the investor must have the discipline to consider selling at least some of his winning positions when the respective stock prices begin approaching their intrinsic values. One fundamental tenet of value investing is that in the long term the market is a weighing machine, i.e., given enough time the market will produce correct prices that approximate the intrinsic values of the underlying businesses. However, in the short term, the market is to a large degree unpredictable. If the crowd is behaving in an irrational manner, it is very difficult to predict the degree of irrationality, or how long the irrationality will last. Thus, either buying stock positions that the investor knows are above intrinsic value, or holding on to existing positions that the investor knows are above intrinsic value, constitutes speculation, not investment.

When an investor is considering selling a current position in which he has a large unrealized gain, his opportunity cost analysis has to consider that any new opportunity must not be just a little better than holding on to his current position, it must be a good bit better. For example, assume that an investor has large unrealized gains in certain stocks, and the stocks have become somewhat fairly priced or fully priced. Here the investor is faced with a decision of whether to sell part or all of these positions, and if he does sell, whether to buy something else or hold cash. Assuming the investor sells his positions and has no unrealized losses to offset his gains, after he pays capital gains tax he is just left with roughly 75% of his capital to either hold in cash or invest in the new opportunity. Assuming that the investor is selling to purchase a new investment, the investor has to believe that his 75% invested in the new position will do better than the 100% invested in the current position. Thus any new opportunities have to be very good. The investor may also want to make a distinction between holdings that he views as permanent positions due to their perceived long-term compounding growth potential, and holdings that were purchase primarily for their bargain price and which lack long-term compounding potential. For example, the investor may want to hold on to certain positions regardless of price, or at least he will require a higher overvaluation threshold to sell these positions. Examples of such long-term compounding companies would include Berkshire Hathaway, Markel, Leucadia, Brookfield Asset Management, etc. At the other end of the spectrum, where the investor has bought a cyclical stock at a bargain price (at the bottom of the cycle), such as an energy stock or commodity-based stock, the investor will likely be better off selling the position at or near the top of the cycle.

Selling fully or overpriced securities during a clear market bubble and holding cash can seemingly be a good idea, as the investor will have dry powder during the inevitable downturn. As such, when the bubble bursts and stocks are again being offered at obscenely low prices, the investor will have the ability to make bargain purchases. On the other hand, it is difficult to time market cycles, and the investor may sell well before the bubble pops, hence losing out on years of stock appreciation. Another strategy to consider for the investor with the intestinal fortitude, and preferably with alternative streams of income, is that if these fairly priced investments have solid long-term prospects and/or are paying good dividends, the investor may hold on to most or all of these investments, and if a downturn occurs use the amount invested as "dry powder" for future purchases in the form of a margin account. In other words, the investor may maintain these fairly priced holdings as collateral for later purchases on margin. One problem with this approach is that in a general stock market decline the values of these investments may go down with the overall market, leaving less value to use for margin purchases. However, as noted above, it is virtually impossible to predict when stock market declines will occur, and hence the benefit of remaining fully invested is that the investor is able to fully participate in the rising market. If there are other identifiable undervalued investment opportunities, the investor is likely better off to remain fully invested, preferably by selling his fairly priced positions for these new opportunities. The general trend of the market is upward, and holding a large percentage of cash for lengthy periods of time can be a serious drag on performance. If the investor's current positions are not merely fairly priced, but in fact are quite overpriced, and he cannot identify undervalued investment opportunities, then he most likely should sell these overpriced positions and hold cash until new opportunities arise.

His second defense is a clear understanding of the crowd psychology at play in the market. Similar to our discussion above regarding maintaining rationality in a macroeconomic crisis, during a stock market bubble the investor must be able to clearly understand and articulate the psychological forces at play that are producing this phenomenon. A stock market bubble is largely a product of "get rich quick syndrome" and greed, with a number of other psychological effects as contributing factors. A good understanding of these factors and how they interact to cause such large-scale irrationality will provide the investor with good ammunition to avoid following the crowd.

First and foremost, the innate desire in all of us to achieve quick and easy wealth will act as a magnet, pulling us in to participate in the market bubble. During a dramatic rise in stock prices, as the average market participant constantly sees those around him getting rich, in particular as portrayed in financial media, it will be hard not to get sucked in with the crowd. The human desire to get rich quick is perhaps best on display in casinos, where people fruitlessly spend money with the hope of the rich strike. The people who gamble at casinos must know that the odds are stacked against them. Regardless, they play on. The stock market is even more psychologically enticing than a casino, especially given the fact that stock market is actually weighted in the investor's favor, i.e., the stock market will almost certainly rise over any extended period of time, lifting all boats in the process. Consider that in a casino over any period of time, such as a few hours or a day, more people will generally be losing than winning. Sure there may be a few people you notice on a "lucky streak,'" and given a long enough period there may even be an occasional "big strike," but in general most people are losing as much or more as they are winning. Unlike casinos, during a bubble in the stock market it appears for a lengthy period of time that *everyone* in the market is winning, and winning big. Consider the equivalent situation in a casino, where a person was gambling in a casino for a very lengthy period of time, such as months or years, and *everyone* appeared to be winning the *entire time*. The person would be absolutely intoxicated with the thought of certain riches, and would not be able to pull himself away from the tables. This phenomenon happens in a stock market bubble – participants see everyone else "winning" (making easy money) and simply cannot pull themselves away.

Combine this with the problems people have with uncertainty, such as recency bias, i.e., the tendency to extrapolate the recent past and current trend with unwarranted confidence, and believe things will continue as they have well into the future. People will naturally view the past rise in stock prices as the way things will be. As discussed previously, people will take a quick glance in their rearview mirror and use this as a guide to the future. Further, a combination of consistency bias, confirmation bias and overconfidence bias will act in concert to virtually assure that the average participant will expect the current market boom to continue indefinitely. Consistency bias is the notion that people desire to be consistent with their past positions and decisions. Confirmation bias causes people to seek out evidence that tends to confirm their currently held views, and to suppress or ignore evidence that is counter to their views. Finally, overconfidence bias causes people to have unwarranted confidence in their own abilities, making them less likely to question their decisions. Each of these biases will reinforce the view of a perpetually rising market. The participant will tend to want to believe that the future of rising stock prices will be consistent with his past purchase actions, the participant will seek out confirming evidence to the exclusion of any pesky evidence of market reversal and hence impending doom, and finally he will have unwarranted confidence in his views.

Consider also the affect heuristic – the happy feeling people have when they are achieving large paper gains in their stockholdings. As noted above, when the stock market is booming, the decision-making process of the average market participant is affected by the easy money being made. The emotional happiness of making quick and easy money tends to trump the more cautious and rational analytical side of his brain. Here the affect heuristic effectively produces a "willing suspension of disbelief" in the mind of the would-be investor, causing him to ignore the high valuations and other evidence of bubble behavior. Instead, due to the participant's extreme emotional liking of easy money, he gets caught up in the euphoria. The end result is that his normal analytical thinking process takes a back seat to the emotional excitement of large easy gains.

As we have discussed, the powerful force of social influence (herd mentality) magnifies the above biases, as the participant takes comfort in being part of the herd. Even more, as analogized above, participating in the stock market during a bubble is akin to gambling at the casino for a lengthy time during which everyone else appears to be winning. It is incredibly hard for the average participant to take his winnings and walk away from the table during such a time.

The intelligent investor who understands these powerful psychological forces at play will be in a much better position to avoid falling in with the maddening crowd. Without this understanding, the investor will be left wondering if his valuation estimates are incorrect. He will wonder why he is so out of touch with the market's evaluation of stock prices. With this understanding, the investor will realize the reasons for the market excesses. He will understand why the market is mispricing stocks, and he will hence be in a much better position to trust his own valuation appraisals rather than falling under the spell of Mr. Market.

A Short Discussion of Risk

Much has been written about the concept of risk in the investing arena. The conventional wisdom in academic circles is that risk can be equated to volatility. More particularly, according to academics the concept of risk for a particular stock is defined as the relative volatility of that stock as compared to the overall market, this measure of risk being expressed by the Greek symbol "beta." In order for this definition of risk to make sense, one must ignore the fact that stock prices represent values of their underlying businesses, and instead focus on stock prices only as mere numbers that wiggle around on charts, and which are part of a larger data set comprising all stock prices. In this make-believe world, the amount by which an individual stock price has historically moved around on a chart, compared to the price movement of the overall data set, defines its future risk.

There are a number of serious problems with this definition of risk, a full discussion of which is beyond the scope of this book. Perhaps the main problem with volatility as a proxy for risk is that this academic theory of risk completely discounts the notion that a company can have an intrinsic value that differs from its stock price. If one accepts the fact that a business CAN have an intrinsic value that differs from its stock price, and that stock prices eventually gravitate towards their correct intrinsic values over the long term, then the entire theory of volatility as risk necessarily fails, since past volatility tells us nothing about whether a security is currently mispriced. In the words of Warren Buffett:

> The riskiness of an investment is *not* measured by beta (a Wall Street term encompassing volatility and often used in measuring risk) but rather by the probability -- the *reasoned* probability -- of that investment causing its owner a loss of purchasing power over his contemplated holding period. Assets can fluctuate greatly in price and not be risky as long as they are reasonably certain to deliver increased purchasing power over their holding period. And as we will see, a nonfluctuating asset can be laden with risk.[45]

If an investor is able to determine an estimate of the intrinsic value of a business, and assuming that the current stock price differs from this estimate of intrinsic value, the investor will thus be able to "know" in some sense the direction of movement of the stock price over the intermediate to long term. We would agree with modern finance theory that in the short term the market is largely unpredictable and the direction of stock prices in the near term are to a large degree erratic and unpredictable. However, Benjamin Graham taught that in the long run the stock market is a weighing machine, meaning that given enough time the price of a stock will converge to (or overshoot) its intrinsic value. Thus perhaps the greatest risk that an investor can have is to NOT consider business valuation as the cornerstone of his investment approach.

In reality, there are two risks that investors really care about. The first risk that an investor cares about is that of losing money, or losing purchasing power. The second, lesser important risk that he cares about is that he will miss out on opportunities – that he will make less money than he thought he would or could have. The value investing literature generally teaches two main approaches to reducing investment risk. First and foremost, the primary tool in the value investor's tool belt to ameliorate risk is to insist on a large margin of safety in his purchase price, i.e., to insist on a large difference between his estimated value of the company and the price he is paying for a piece of the company. This greatly reduces risk on a number of fronts. First, it reduces the risk of permanent loss of capital when the investor is wrong about his calculations of valuation. Put simply, the greater the margin of safety, the less chance there will be permanent loss should the investor turn out to be wrong. In addition, securities that are greatly undervalued are less likely drop precipitously during a market downturn. As discussed previously, the intrinsic value of the business acts somewhat like a magnet on stock prices, and if the investor has purchased a stock at a price well below intrinsic value, it is unlikely (but certainly not impossible) to fall that much further. The investor's second tool to ameliorate risk is to purchase solid businesses with good cash flow, good return on equity, and solid management and capital allocation. Buying great businesses also operates to reduce risk, since businesses that reliably produce good cash flow and have these other desirable characteristics are generally less affected in a market downturn than companies which do not. Further, great businesses with a good return on equity are likely to do well over the long term regardless of market cycles. Such great businesses are also less sensitive to the initial purchase price due to their ability to compound at high rates of return over many years.

As a side note, the investor may also be willing to take on an aspect of the second risk above (making less money than he thought he would or could) in order to reduce the first risk (of losing money or purchasing power). This brings us back to our discussion of when to sell fairly priced or overpriced securities. When the investor holds securities that are fairly priced or overpriced, he will likely consider selling them even as they continue to rise in price with the overall market. Here the investor is assuming some of the second risk (making less money than perhaps he could have) in order to reduce his first risk (of losing money). Of course, a large part of the sell decision involves opportunity costs of other prospective investments. If the investor has one or more equity positions that he believes are fair to overpriced, and he cannot find suitable investments, then the investor should likely sell and begin to hold cash.

This book offers a third way to ameliorate risk – using an understanding of the wisdom and folly of the crowd to help guide stock selection. In particular, if the investor insists that an "inefficient rationale" be present in each of his investment decisions, this will go a long way in reducing his risk, i.e., in reducing the risk of permanent loss of capital. Due to: 1) the powerful force of crowd wisdom; 2) the extremely reliable tendency of human nature to depart from crowd wisdom when certain conditions are present; and 3) the notion that stock mispricings for the most part only occur when crowd wisdom criteria are lacking, i.e., when there is some type of inefficient rationale, the investor who consistently bases his decisions on the presence of an inefficient rationale will have less risk in his investment decisions, i.e., less chance of being wrong.

11. QUANTIFYING THE FOOLISHNESS OF THE CROWD AND ITS EFFECT ON CORRECT STOCK PRICES

We have seen that, due to the "wisdom of the crowd", when a large number of people apply their judgment to a particular estimate or result, and certain criteria are present, the underlying "wisdom" of the crowd will manifest. However, when the collective judgments of the crowd are skewed by irrationality and/or systemic forces, the resulting output from the crowd will not be wisdom, but instead will be a result that is offset from this normal wisdom (the "Foolish Offset"). The question posed here is whether it would be possible for one to study and understand the nature of this irrationality sufficiently to predict, or at least estimate, the degree of this Foolish Offset. In other words, how quantifiable is the Foolishness of the crowd, i.e., to what degree, or to what accuracy, can the investor determine the amount of offset from the correct stock price produced by market irrationality?

Here it must be admitted that this offset cannot be determined with any degree of precision. Recall from the earlier discussion in Chapter 2 where the "correct stock price" was described as corresponding to the intrinsic value of a business. We defined the intrinsic value of a business as the value a well informed and rational private buyer would pay for the business with knowledge of all available information and conducted in an arms-length transaction, with neither side being under duress to buy or sell. However, the concept of intrinsic value itself cannot be calculated with any precision. Benjamin Graham characterized the concept of intrinsic value in the following manner:

> We must recognize, however, that intrinsic value is an elusive concept. In general terms it is understood to be that value which is justified by the facts, e.g., the assets, earnings, dividends, definite prospects, as distinct, let us say, from market quotations established by artificial manipulation or distorted by psychological excesses. But it is a great mistake to imagine that intrinsic value is as definite and as determinable as is the market price.[48]

Graham also wisely noted that one does not have to determine an exact number for intrinsic value. Rather, an estimate of intrinsic value in a range that clearly demonstrates that it is well above the current stock price is sufficient to justify a purchase of the stock. As Graham said:

> The essential point is that security analysis does not seek to determine exactly what is the intrinsic value of a given security. It needs only to establish either that the value is *adequate* – e.g., to protect a bond or to justify a stock purchase – or else that the value is considerably higher or considerably lower than the market price. For such purposes an indefinite and approximate measure of intrinsic value may be sufficient. To use a homely simile, it is quite possible to decide by inspection that a woman is old enough to vote without knowing her age or that a man is heavier than he should be without knowing his exact weight.

Graham further acknowledged that the concept of intrinsic value was flexible, and the range of possible intrinsic values could vary based upon the degree of uncertainty in the particular circumstances. For example, if there were a greater amount of uncertainty in appraising the intrinsic value of a particular business situation, the range of potential intrinsic values would increase accordingly due to this inherent uncertainty. However, this wider range of possible intrinsic values could still justify a purchase decision if the current stock price was still well below the minimum appraised intrinsic value within the assessed range. Hence, when there is uncertainty in appraising the intrinsic value of the business, an investor should consider a larger range of possible intrinsic values to account for this uncertainty, knowing that the current stock price needs to be considerably lower than the lowest value in this range to provide an adequate margin of safety and thus justify purchase of the respective stock. In discussing this concept in Security Analysis, Graham provides several different examples of the appraisal of the intrinsic value of a business with different degrees of uncertainty, noting that if the current stock price is well below the lowest value in the assessed range, however large that range may be, purchase of the underlying stock would have been justified. Graham then comments:

> This should indicate how flexible is the concept of intrinsic value as applied to security analysis. Our notion of the intrinsic value may be more or less distinct, depending on the particular case. The degree of indistinctness may be expressed by a very hypothetical 'range of approximate value,' which would grow wider as the uncertainty of the picture increased . . . . It would follow that even a very indefinite idea of the intrinsic value may still justify a conclusion if the current price falls far outside either the maximum or minimum appraisal.

The assessment of the Foolishness of the Crowd would follow a very similar line of thinking. The current degree of Foolishness or irrationality in the stock market, and more particularly its influence on current stock prices, is not susceptible to quantification, but at best can be assessed as a possible range of values. Throughout modern finance one sees the attempt to quantify parameters, such as risk, value, etc., that are simply not quantifiable. As Charlie Munger has said, modern finance seems to suffer from Physics Envy – an envy of the ability in hard sciences such as physics to quantify values with precision. This ability to quantify in the hard sciences is primarily due to the nature of hard sciences. Certain values, such as the speed of light, the gravity of the earth, the ratio of a circle's circumference to its diameter (pi), are both determinable and quantifiable, and experiments can be repeatedly performed to verify the accuracy of this quantification. This is simply not possible to a large degree in the soft sciences. There are simply too many factors and variables at play, experiments cannot be repeated under the same operating conditions since conditions change, and most importantly, the output of a financial marketplace (prices) is heavily subject to human psychology and emotion.

The degree of accuracy in assessing this Foolish Offset (the effect of irrationality on stock prices) is almost certainly less, and likely quite a bit less, than the degree of certainty in assessing intrinsic value. Estimation of intrinsic value is based on a number of objective or quantitative criteria such as prior and current earnings, cash flow, assets, capital structure and debt ratio, price to earnings (P/E) ratio, price to book (P/B) ratio, etc., as well as a number of subjective or qualitative criteria, such as quality of management, predicted earnings growth, competitive position, and overall business prospects.

Estimation of the degree of Foolishness of the Crowd, namely how large the investor perceives the degree of irrationality to be in the market, would seemingly be based largely on subjective or qualitative factors. These qualitative factors would include: 1) knowledge of financial history; 2) personal experience with past market cycles; 3) a studied and thoughtful analysis of current events; and 4) knowledge of market psychology and irrationality and its effect on the wisdom of the crowd (the subject of this book). The intelligent investor should be able to put this knowledge and experience together to arrive at a rough estimate of the degree of irrationality, and hence the degree of mispricing, in the market.

Recently, certain quantitative assessments have been developed which attempt to estimate the degree of irrationality in the market. In particular, several indexes have recently been created which purportedly show the amount of fear and/or greed in the market. For example, the Chicago Board Options Exchange has created the Market Volatility Index, referred to as the VIX. The VIX is a measure of the implied volatility of a wide range of S&P 500 index options and thus represents one measure of the market's expectation of stock market volatility over the next 30 day period. The VIX provides insight on investor's expectations of future market volatility, which is presumed to correlate with investor fear and uncertainty. Hence the VIX is often referred to as the *fear index* or the *fear gauge*. CNN Money has also created a "Fear & Greed Index" which purports to show which emotion is currently driving the market. The Fear & Greed Index is calculated based on seven indicators, such as stock price momentum, stock price strength, the put/call ratio, and market volatility (as measured by the VIX), among other factors. The Fear & Greed index attempts to indicate the level of fear and/or greed that is currently in the market. It could be that one of these indexes, or perhaps some combination of them, could be used to provide a quantitative value useful in assessing, or perhaps even indicating, the relative amount of fear or greed, and hence a measure of the degree of irrationality, in the marketplace. This topic should probably best be left to some enterprising graduate student in behavioral finance.

Regardless, estimation of the effect of irrationality on stock prices will necessarily be imprecise. Perhaps the best that can be said on the subject is to use the various qualitative factors mentioned above, perhaps most importantly our knowledge of the various causes of the Foolishness of the Crowd, to attempt to estimate the degree of under or overvaluation (the degree of mispricing) that is occurring in the market due to this irrationality. It may be that in all cases such an estimation can only produce a single binary result, this being either that the current Foolishness of the Crowd is currently distorting stock prices, or a particular stock price, to a large degree, or it is not. Even this result would be quite useful to the investor as an aid in supporting his fundamental analysis. For example, this additional insight into why current stock prices are at current levels may perhaps provide the investor with the necessary courage to take large positions in clearly underpriced securities. However, it seems likely that the estimation of the current Foolish effect on stock prices can produce better than a binary result. In particular, it seems quite likely that one may be able to qualitatively assess the degree of mispricing which is currently present in the market well beyond a simple binary value. Here it seems that the investor's understanding of current events, his knowledge of financial history, his personal experience with past market cycles, and his knowledge of the Foolishness of the Crowd, will be the best guide to estimations of the degree of irrationality in the market.

Fundamental analysis will also of course be useful here, in conjunction with the user's qualitative assessment of the current Foolishness in the market, to help confirm the estimated degree of mispricing in the market. More specifically, fundamental analysis may be used to assess the intrinsic values of at least some of the businesses that are the object of the current irrationality. A survey of the differences between the intrinsic value estimates of various businesses and current stock prices may be very helpful in confirming the investor's estimate of both the current degree of irrationality and the current level of mispricing in the stock market. Once the investor has some estimation of the degree of mispricing in the market, based on his qualitative estimate of market irrationality and his fundamental analysis of a few select companies, the investor can be fairly confident that a large number of similarly situated companies are likely also mispriced.

CONCLUSION

The wisdom of the crowd is a powerful force in many areas of human endeavor. When certain criteria are met, the average of the opinions or estimates from a large sample set of people is virtually certain to be a very good result, better than any individual expert could produce. Despite the discussion in this book of the "Foolishness of the Crowd", the concept of crowd wisdom deserves a considerable amount of respect, even in financial markets. In fact, the investing philosophy in this book is largely based on the strength of the wisdom of the crowd, coupled with the predictability of crowd behavior and psychology, which reliably produces offsets from that wisdom under certain conditions. We know the wisdom of the crowd will tend to produce correct stock prices when the relevant crowd wisdom criteria are present. We also know that human nature is extremely reliable, perhaps the one constant in an ever changing world. When certain conditions are present human nature will reliably produce irrational behavior, and this irrational behavior results in the "Foolish Offset" from the normal crowd wisdom. Thus the wisdom of the crowd and the Foolish Offset are both extremely reliable phenomena, and together they create the perfect recipe for determining stock mispricing. In fact, due to the large degree of wisdom present in a financial marketplace under most circumstances, a Foolish Offset (some type of identifiable crowd or systemic irrationality) is almost required to be present for a mispricing to occur.

We propose an investment framework that relies on three separate aspects or "legs" to establish a great investment, these being 1) the variant perception; 2) the inefficient rationale; and 3) cloning evidence (the wisdom of a select crowd). First, the investor should apply fundamental-based valuation principles to determine a valuation for a business that is the subject of the investment. If the investor's valuation is considerably above the current market price, producing a suitable "margin of safety", then the investment is likely a good one. This is classic value investing 101. The investor's valuation that differs markedly from the market price is referred to here as the variant perception – the investor's perception of the value of a business which is at variance with that of the market. Second, the investor should be able to develop an "inefficient rationale" as to why this mispricing exists in the market. The inefficient rationale will be predicated on some aspect of the wisdom of the crowd criteria being lacking in some notable aspect, typically being a result of crowd psychology or herd behavior, usually involving fear, greed and/or uncertainty. Various systemic constraints in the marketplace may also play a factor in mispricing. Due to the predictable reliability of human nature, the presence of an inefficient rationale is perhaps the best indicator of stock mispricing, in many cases even better than the investor's own valuation analysis (variant perception). Third, the investor should take advantage of the wisdom of a truly wise crowd by studying and selectively cloning the investments of other respected value investors. The investments made by other successful value investors are worthy of study, and they are useful both as a shortcut to finding potential bargains as well as confirming evidence that the investor's variant perception and inefficient rational are sound.

When all three legs of this investment framework are strongly present, the proposed investment will most likely be extremely sound and worthy of a high conviction investment. When only two of the legs are present, the investment may still be a good one, but it will likely merit less of a commitment than if all three legs were present. If the investor cannot articulate an inefficient rationale for a proposed investment, then the investor should be very cautious, as here he is essentially betting that he is smarter than, or is more knowledgeable than, the market. This is typically not a good bet. The investor who adheres to this investment framework essentially places the full benefit of crowd wisdom and knowledge into his corner, including both the wisdom of the crowd and predictable departures from this wisdom. To the investor schooled in wisdom of the crowd criteria, these predictable departures act as signposts for great investments. In closing, the investor who has the patience and fortitude to follow this investment framework will be richly rewarded.

(Endnotes)

1 Benjamin Graham and David Dodd, *Security Analysis* 6th Edition, pg. 106

2 Benjamin Graham and David Dodd, *Security Analysis* 6th Edition, pg. 107

3 Benjamin Graham and David Dodd, *Security Analysis* 6th Edition, pg. 106

4 Benjamin Graham and David Dodd, *Security Analysis* 6th Edition, pgs 69-70

5 Galton, F., "Vox Populi", *Nature*, March 7, 1907

6 "The Ballot Box", *Nature*, March 28, 1907

7 Nature, Vol. 35, No. 1952 (3/28/07) from footnote 26 of Wikipedia article on Francis Galton

8 The author vividly remembers reading this story a long time ago, but alas cannot remember where it came from, nor can he locate this story on the Internet

9 "The Wisdom of Crowds" (Vox Populi) by Francis Galton; *http://www.all-about-psychology.com/the-wisdom-of-crowds.html*

10 Berkshire Hathaway 1988 Shareholder Letter

11 Berkshire Hathaway 1988 Shareholder Letter

12 Benjamin Graham, a quote attributed to Graham by Warren Buffett; 1993 Berkshire Hathaway shareholder letter; see also *Security Analysis* Sixth Edition chapter 39, pg. 497

13 Howard Marks. *The Most Important Thing.* Columbia University Press; 2011-03-23. pgs. 111-112

14 Berk and De Marzo, *Corporate Finance 3rd Edition*; Chapter 3

15 Randy Cohen, Christopher Polk, and Bernhard Silli, "Best Ideas; March 18, 2009 *http://ssrn.com/abstract=1364827*

16 John Maynard Keynes *The General Theory of Employment, Interest and Money* Book 4, Chapter 12, Section 5, p. 158

17 Peter Lynch *One Up on Wall Street* pg. 59

18 Lorenz, et al. "How Social Influence can Undermine the Wisdom of the Crowd Effect" Proceedings of the National Academy of Sciences of the

United States of America; May 31, 2011; vol. 108 no. 22; 9020-9025 *http://www.pnas.org/content/108/22/9020.full.*

19   Lorenz, et al. "How Social Influence can Undermine the Wisdom of the Crowd Effect" Proceedings of the National Academy of Sciences of the United States of America; May 31, 2011; vol. 108 no. 22; 9020-9025; Abstract *http://www.pnas.org/content/108/22/9020.full.*

20   Mark Buchanan "The Wisdom (???) of Crowds" The Physics of Finance, July 22, 2011 *http://physicsoffinance.blogspot.com/2011/07/wisdom-of-crowds.html.*

21   Peter Lynch "One Up on Wall Street" pg. 56

22   See Gallup Economy, April 20, 2011 *http://www.gallup.com/poll/147206/stock-market-investments-lowest-1999.aspx*

23   Seth A. Klarman Preface to *Security Analysis*, 6th edition by Benjamin Graham and David Dodd, pg. xxi

24   Peter Lynch, *One Up on Wall Street* pg. 64

25   MarketWatch interview with David Blitzer, chairman of the S&P index committee; March 28, 2004 *http://www.marketwatch.com/story/sp-move-to-float-adjusted-indexes-will-create-turnover*

26   Horizon Research Group, "The Owner-Operator Company: A Superior Business Model"

27   Humphrey Neill, *The Art of Contrary Thinking*, 6th Edition 2010, pgs. 51-52

28   Humphrey Neill, *The Art of Contrary Thinking*, 6th Edition 2010, pg. 52

29   Student Visit; May 6, 2005; URL: *http://boards.fool.com/buffettjayhawk-qa-22736469.aspx?sort=whole#22803680;*

30   Jason Zweig, *Your Money and Your Brain* Chapter 3 pgs. 34-52

31   Howard Marks, *The Most Important Thing* Columbia University Press, 2011-03-23 Chapter 8, pg. 102

32   Philip Fisher *Common Stocks and Uncommon Profits;* pg. 91

33   Student Visit; May 6, 2005; URL: *http://boards.fool.com/buffettjayhawk-qa-22736469.aspx?sort=whole#22803680;*

34   Edward C. Johnson II, "Contrary Opinion in Stock Market Techniques", published in *Classics: An Investor's Anthology*, edited by Charles D. Ellis, pgs. 392-398

35 Howard Marks *The Most Important Thing*, Columbia University Press, 2011-03-23. pg. 95

36 Howard Marks *The Most Important Thing*. Columbia University Press, 2011-03-23. pgs. 111-112

37 Michael Steinhardt, *No Bull—My Life In and Out of Markets*, pg. 191

38 Michael Steinhardt, No Bull—My Life In and Out of Markets, pg. 129

39 Steinhardt   on   Variant   Perception,   interview   with   Charlie Rose;   interview   2766;   *http://deepvaluestocks.wordpress.com/2011/05/23/ steinhardt-on-variant-perception/*

40 San Francisco Business Times June 13, 2012 "Former Wells Fargo CEO Dick Kovacevich blasts TARP: An 'unmitigated disaster'" *http://www.bizjournals. com/sanfrancisco/blog/2012/06/wells-fargo-dick-kovacevich-occupy-tarp.html?page=all*

41 The author acknowledges the outstanding and thoughtful research of Horizon Kinetics, Horizon Research Group, for certain of the ideas expressed in this section, specifically the publication titled "Indexation as a Business", originally published in the Devil's Advocate Report Compendium, January 2012

42 Bruce Berkowitz interview on Consuelo Mack Wealthtrack, #916 2012/10/12

43 Benjamin Graham *The Intelligent Investor* Chapter 8, pg. 189

44 John O'Farrell, An Utterly Impartial History of Britain - Or 2000 Years of Upper Class Idiots In Charge (October 22, 2007) (2007, Doubleday, ISBN 978-0-385-61198-5)

45 Warren Buffett: Why Stocks Beat Gold and Bonds Fortune Magazine,   February   9,   2012   *http://finance.fortune.cnn.com/2012/02/09/ warren-buffett-berkshire-shareholder-letter/*

46 Benjamin Graham and David Dodd, *Security Analysis* 6th edition pg. 64

www.ingramcontent.com/pod-product-compliance
Lightning Source LLC
Chambersburg PA
CBHW060015210326
41520CB00009B/894